T0209400

Beyond The Gate of
GLORY

SEQUEL TO *THROUGH THE GATE OF GLORY*

Ron Hobden

BEYOND THE GATE OF GLORY
SEQUEL TO THROUGH THE GATE OF GLORY

iUniverse books may be ordered through booksellers or by contacting:

iUniverse
1663 Liberty Drive
Bloomington, IN 47403
www.iuniverse.com
844-349-9409

ISBN: 978-1-6632-5263-0 (sc)
ISBN: 978-1-6632-5264-7 (e)

Library of Congress Control Number: 2023907639

Print information available on the last page.

iUniverse rev. date: 04/21/2023

As we reminisce over the decades of service to our Lord, we trust that you will find our adventures interesting. May you feel God's Holy Spirit alive within you. We were blessed in God's calling both my wife Elaine and me into our forty years of pastoral ministry. Now after our 65th wedding anniversary, I will share some of the experiences we have enjoyed, others we have endured as recorded in my diary. Then also my envisioning of how it might have unfolded had I been called to Glory earlier in life. Should you encounter times of stress, Know HE is there as the Psalmist assures.

> *Because he holds fast to me in love, I will*
> *deliver him; I will protect him, because he*
> *knows my name. When he calls to me, I will*
> *answer him; I will be with him in trouble; I*
> *will rescue him and honor him. With long life*
> *I will satisfy him and show him my salvation.*
> Ps. 91:14 – 16

Early in my teen life I began to record diary entries. This practice continued throughout my various endeavors. Beginning in 1956

a general labourer	years
Provincial Court Officer	years
O.P.P.	years,
Judicial Officer	years
University studies	years
Off Campus	(6 years)
Pastoral Duties	years
Retirement 2020 age –	years

Introduction

According to our understanding of our Lord and Saviour, it is our belief that the vast majority of life experiences are not manipulated by Him, but that He always stands ready to intervene, to cause or allow, life-enrichment and guidance from and through one's joyful, terrifying, sad, humorous and even those boring experiences. Therefore, every 'happening' in our lives can be, if allowed, and, in accordance with our free will, an opportunity for the Holy Spirit to be our guide and strength.

Early in our Christian walk the words of Joshua become embedded within us. Let us suggest that when challenges come your way that these words can be your compass;

"Then you will know which way to go, since you have never been this way before." Joshua 3:4

While the mention of a soul's arrival at judgement, then, met and guided by saints who have passed from judgement to Glory, may not be in complete harmony with Holy Word, neither, as I share our past sixty-five years of service, can I find conflict within the pages of scripture. May I share my *Adventures of Thought* and Reality with my readers. These 'adventures' range from pages in my diary" to illustrations of how possible meetings could take place in Glory with family, friends, saints already in Glory.

Ronald Hobden

He Bitted Me

Dear Jesus

Thank you, Lord, that in your wisdom, You, the great physician, knows when to encourage our memory that we might right certain wrongs, or, might be freed from psychological damage. Lord, as a young teen, newly made part of Your family, I questioned Your promise from Psalms 121 that you watched over me. I was reminded:

"There I was, a four-year-old toddler", As I have no recollection of the event, I rely on others for affirmation, that I had not approached, nor threatened the dog, but suddenly he attacked. After freeing me from the animal's jaws, it was apparent that my very survival was in question. "Lord, that's when You stepped in:"

Eyes were drawn to dust on the River Road. A car! an uncle ran out flagged down the car, a taxi. "He needs to get to the hospital." As during these war years, gas was strictly rationed, the taxi driver shook his head, I do not have enough gas to get there. Seeing my condition, he said,

"Get in, I should have enough gas to get us there. We will worry about getting home later." Several bandages, one hundred and forty stitches later, thank you Jesus, we actually made the return trip home with our remaining gas.

I Love You Lord – Ron

W.W. 2

As Nazism declared war upon humanity, father's sense of patriotism inspired him to enlist. Upon dad's training completed he received a pre-embarkation leave, to say 'farewell' to wife and family before heading overseas into combat. It was just an hour before dad was to catch a train for home that he received a summons to attend his commanding officer. "Hobden", the C.O. questioned, "I have no record of a baptismal certificate in your file." "But sir, I am not a church person, I was never baptized". Shaking his head, the commanding officer replied; "Upon your return from this leave, you SHALL present to me a copy of a baptismal certificate." My father's only response, in that era; "Yes sir." Years later after my parents had a personal relationship with Jesus, Mom and Dad told of their search to find, as they said; "a reverend" who would follow the base commander's order. How they scanned the telephone directory, made a phone call and the following morning we all entered the minister's office. Paper work completed the cleric pointing toward me questioning, "has the child been done?" At mom's affirming that I had not 'been done', the minister replied; "Well I'll do the kid for the same price." So, with the 'dampening' of my curls, I was reportedly, ushered into the 'family of God". Later in life I was to question my "baptism".

I Love You Lord - Ron

The Apostle

Dear Jesus

The ten days passed all too quickly as father bid farewell. The next day, mother accepted a supper invitation to my uncle's. At the end of the evening noting mother's anxiety about heading home to an empty house, uncle accompanied us. Upon his leaving, mother being apprehensive, locked the bedroom door. Several minutes passed then, a noise as the outline of a figure crawled from under the bed. In absolute terror mother held her breath, as the intruder unlocked the door and left. We caught the morning bus to Massey and Grandma and Grandpa Gambles.

It was said about Grandma Gamble that she was slight in stature but mighty when riled. One afternoon an 'apostle' of a well-known cult paid us a visit. Noticing mother and me, he asked if there was a father. When mother said that dad was overseas with the military, the cultist went berserk. Dancing around, he started spieling that my dad was a murderer, a butcher, pointing his hands, chanting; "Bang –Bang – you're dead." Grandma's fury was ignited. Grabbing a broom, she started beating the crazed cultist over the head. After a few vicious jabs into his chest, one into his neck, his falling off the deck backwards, he fled to his car from what was to be his final visit. Now, many years have passed but thank you Lord for these precious memories.

I Love you Lord – Ron

The Isle De France

Dear Jesus:

Even though I was just a three year old when Dad went off to war and now well into the third year later, I remember so well, so clearly, my mother sitting on the floor, pages of the newspaper all around her as she pointed to the various ships that had docked and the list of soldiers names on board.

Suddenly she gasped. "Your father"! Look. the Isle De France, He's coming home". Mom pointed out the ship then among hundreds of names, LOOK – Russell Hobden." There he is"!

Three days later a convoy of vehicles, horns blaring as uncles, aunts, cousins and even strangers embarked from the flotilla. Then someone I was supposed to know, first held mother in his arms then reached out to me. Thus, it was that I was reintroduced to my 'father'.

One of my greatest blessings was the brief time it took for my reintroduction to and my acceptance of the stranger who suddenly 'broke' into our family and this stranger was my father.

The year was 1947, dad working at INCO in Sudbury. With mother's approval, purchased a farm sixty miles to the west just south of Massey on the shore of the Spanish River. Thus it was that I said farewell to my classmates, knowing that up to this time school just a 'stone's throw from home has become a mile and a half trek.

It's no matter I Love You Lord – Ron

My Culinary Efforts

Warm in summer, not so warm in minus degrees during winter months. How peaceful it was. As dad was working away from home, the following year I was introduced to milking the cows! Sans milking machines I was introduced to the 'pull and squeeze" method and soon it was five of the nine cows for mother, four for me and we'd alternate the following milking. Following milking we would prepare a device called a separator to remove the cream from the milk, then carefully stow the cream until the day the truck arrived to transport it to the creamery.

Things were going well for our family. Dad was home for a few days and I decided that I would show off my newly acquired baking skills. An hour and a half later I marched out the door and headed over to where Mom and Dad where fencing. What's in the box, Mom called, Wait and see I answered. Opening the box, I produced a pair of cake plates. As they held the plates I proudly cut and presented mom first then dad with my masterpiece, a slice of brilliant gold coloured cake with a heap of bright orange icing.

Mother sampled my accomplishment. However Dad's look of bewilderment said it all Yet his, "I think I'll pass, but, thank you anyway. It would be months later when I would again attempt to make it as a baker. This time however it was a white cake with chocolate icing. This time my culinary effort was appreciated. I Love You Lord – Ron

Ruptured Appendix

Dear Jesus:

The doctor said a ruptured appendix. An operation was necessary. For the next three days, I was in the hospital in Espanola beyond the range of our horse and wagon, demanding a return taxi fare home. Fortunately, Aunt Olga offered dad a cot. Immediately following my surgery, the doctor informed dad that all was well however I should remain in the hospital until the bill was paid. Dad, upon heading out to the highway to hitch-hike home, by luck OR God's design, was picked up by a farmer living on the River Road. There was no way he could think of how to come up with the money. "O Lord Jesus, he prayed; Please Lord. help me with this problem I'm facing." Just after lunch, dad walked into town to pick up a few groceries. The store owner noticed that all did not seem to be well with my dad. "Russell, what's the matter?" Dad mentioned his dilemma, "How much do you need?" the grocer asked. "Well," your dad answered "The hospital wants one hundred and ninety-seven dollars. I'll have to sell a cow." "No, I do not think that, at all is right. Listen, I've known you for years, I'd like to just loan you the money, you can pay it back whenever you can. Just a moment." Returning from his office the grocer counted two hundred and fifty dollars into dad's outstretched hand.

That afternoon, dad paid the 'ransom' and set me free. I Love You Lord – Ron

The Sick Cow."

Dear Jesus

It's a couple of months until harvest and there just isn't any work locally for dad, anywhere. This morning, I found Nel one of our nine cows, lying out in the pasture in obvious great distress. There was nothing to do but call the vet. "Jesus, I asked; is there a miracle drug for her?" A few hours later the vet arrived. Accompanied by dad and me, walked out in the field where Nel was lying. Without stopping, he circled the cow, looked into your dad's eyes and said just seven words; "She's going to die, twenty dollars please."

Father was devastated, as he handed over his last twenty. The vet got into his car and drove off. In great sadness at our family's loss I must report that some hours later the vet's prediction came to be. Lord, please help me to understand. I remember her as a calf, I called her Della. Out in the pasture she would come to me and give me a friendly nuzzle. Noticing it was time for supper, I knew instinctively that it would be, Sage Balls. Later I would learn the "truth" about our favoured meal, sage balls.

Please help dad to know how to deal with this, Please Lord, PLEASE! - But Lord, however this turns out we love You, Help us to sense Your leading.

I love You Lord – Ron

Hunting

Dear Jesus:

I finished milking, then after storing the cream for tomorrow's shipment and cleaning up, I headed to the house, picked up dad's 38/55 rifle and headed to the back field. There, just ahead, four white tailed deer were grazing.

Quietly, I crawled on hands and knees, then waited. Watched as the critters made their way toward me. Finally, I chose a large buck, less than fifty meters away, A clear shot, venison on the table tonight! Carefully I sighted, as I began to put pressure on the rifle's trigger, the animal looked up and in my direction. Lord it was that very moment that you answered last evening's question about meat on the table, I was struck on the majesty of that animal. To this day, I can see that buck's majestic eyes staring into my soul. I thought for a moment. We really don't need that meat, why should I take his life?" I lowered the rifle. From that moment sixty-eight years ago, while I have been an avid hunter, my weapon is my camera.

This after noon I would add a few more of nature's beauty to my collection Now I have no quarrel with hunters which includes family members. But as for me, I relish the collection of photos in my albums. Thank You Lord for such a great lesson that day.

I Love You Lord - Ron

Aunt Sarah

Dear Jesus

I remembered Aunt Sarah.so well that as a child, I was among those, privileged to call this gentle child of God 'Aunt Sarah.' We lived on opposite sides of the Spanish River. I was a farm boy on the north side of the Spanish, she on an Indian reservation on the south. Contrary to modern trends, Aunt Sarah proclaimed that she was proud to be called an 'Indian'. I recalled her stating emphatically that she had little time for anyone who attempted to gain fame or fortune through semantics. She always had time to pat me on my head, to inquire about my day, and there were always cookies! She made no excuses that she loved her Lord.

One day in my mid-teens, 'Aunt' Sarah's usual greeting changed; She saw me coming, opened the door and called out; "Welcome preacher." She had heard that I had preached during our young people's service. As I was about to leave, she said, 'Oh, just a moment, I have something to show you." Holding up her well-worn Bible; I want you to have this after I'm gone." Sadly, due to marriage, then moving away from the area, I was never to receive this precious gift.

Yet memories lasted throughout life and on here into my eternity.

How I regretted I was so far away. I was unable to attend her funeral. Even then was I was comforted that I would see her again.

I Love You Lord - Ron

She hasn't REALLY Left Us

Dear Jesus:

One evening after failing to appear for a couple of days, a concerned granddaughter discovered Aunt Sarah lying on her kitchen floor. The doctor was called and declared that her time had come. The following afternoon, the Call to Worship, was followed by a hymn, during which Aunt Sarah sat up in her coffin.

Screams and panic ensued as the terrified congregation burst out of the little church. The doctor admitted that she must have been in a deep coma. Six months would pass before she was again discovered motionless in her cabin. This time the doctor was extremely cautious and after a number of tests declared that there was no doubt! She had passed away.

She was transported to a funeral home where embalming took place and the funeral, went off without a hitch. "Lord, Aunt Sarah was not endowed with beauty! Those who didn't know her were overheard to say she resembled a cartoon witch. Yet all who knew her, and I was most blessed to have been in that number, saw an inner beauty and faith, likened to a heavenly angel. Heavenly Father, thank you for enriching my life and countless others through 'Aunt Sarah". How blessed will be the moments of our first reuniting in Glory! Thinking of her earthly 'beauty", I wait for the moment when I see her Glory beauty. I Love You Lord – Ron

Stick With Me

Dear Jesus:

"At age sixteen when I told Elaine to stick with me and we will go places she never envisioned, she could not have even imagined in her wildest dreams that it would involve, sleeping out in the open in minus 45 degrees on a northern rescue mission, shark fishing in the Caribbean, caught in snowstorms while climbing the Rockies? Piloting our plane when I became ill. Serving as safety officer on our underwater diving team or helping pack my parachutes.

We have certainly had many fun-times in the past sixty-five years of marriage. We've stood on the mountain tops. We have also walked through many dark valleys. We have learned to shout out to Him in praise, to cry out to Him in despair and always we have found He never deserted us, was ALWAYS at our side. To our shame and sorrow, we admit that there were occasions, many, too many when we took our Lord for granted. Forgive us Lord and thank you for Your never forgetting us.

I had been fortunate to have witnessed some of the most breath-taking views on earth. From the Rocky Mountains outside my back window to the beaches of Mexico. O Lord, the magnificence of Your creation is beyond comprehension.

I Love You Lord – Ron

Teen Preacher

Dear Jesus:

I'm ready for my first assignment. For the next three months I'll share the preaching on our seven-point charge with a student from seminary. One Sunday he takes on four of our churches while I visit the remaining three. The next Sunday, we alternate. Dear Jesus; will anyone come to church when the preacher is a sixteen year old kid?

Well my 11:00 a.m. service at Massey was well attended. However at Nairn. for the 2:00 p.m. meeting there wasn't a car in the parking lot. Later in the week, I learned that the Nairn church council had determined that summer services would commence on the second Sunday. Later I would receive a 'heart-felt' apology for not sending notice.

The evening service at Walford was well attended and at the service's end, Mom and Dad, were the last ones out the door, I shall always remember my father's words; "Ron, we are very proud of you". Thankyou Lord, for today, but I need Your guidance through the summer as I prepared for today's challenge I recalled Aunt Sarah's word and turned to Timothy.

*"Let no one despise you for your youth, but set
the believers an example in speech, in conduct.*
1 Timothy 4:12

Holy Spirit, empower me to meet the challenges of life
and be worthy of Your guidance.

I love you Lord – Ron

"Golly" in Glory

Dear Jesus:

About Golly in Glory? Thank you for drawing my attention to the question on my visit to the library. I felt both relieved and excited as I read that I was not alone in my thinking. People far more prominent in the faith, Lord, even spiritual giants declare, affirm their belief that they shall be reunited with their favourite pets in Glory.

I read that there are famous Christian authors who believe that pets go to heaven, including: C. S. Lewis, Peter Kreeft, Sylvia Brown, Niki Bairiki's, Shanahan, James Herriot, and dozens and dozens of others; The list of Christian pastors, theologians, and clergy is lengthy! However, it must be noted that we don't have biblical assurance as to whether or not our pets will be in Glory, I urge the more important question is; will WE be in heaven? It is pointless to ponder the question of whether your pet goes to heaven if you, are not there. Make certain you meet the criteria. As for pets being in heaven or not, the only way for us to find out, is to go there ourselves. Lord may my ministry be in line, in harmony with Your holy word.

Some thank Him for the flow'rs that grow
Some for the stars that shine
My heart is filled with joy and praise
Because I know He's mine

I Love You Lord – Ron

GOLLY – Our Family Friend

Piper Tri-Pacer

May Day

Dear Jesus

Several years have passed, I had kept my diary up to date. A diary that was lost somehow in the confusion of relocating into homes across a few provinces, into the northern region of our land and to our decade in Japan. It seems that I feel led to resume the habit. May my memory be sufficient for the task. And may I have forgiveness for any duplicating of my former books.

As I recall back in the mid to late sixties, a flight from home to Nelson House generated a multitude of prayers first for our survival and later for those prayers being answered. How we thanked the Lord for seeing us through.

Having only a thousand-kilometre range and with uncertain weather in our path. I stopped in Marathon to top up the tanks. While an attendant was fuelling, my weather check indicated heavy headwinds but nothing of concern. About thirty minutes out of Marathon, a fuel gauge caught my attention. We had used almost a quarter of our fuel. As that was doubtful, I wondered if the attendant had not topped off both tanks. In a matter of seconds, the light drizzle turned into a torrent, the wind directly in front. After fifteen minutes in near zero visibility, it was now impossible for me to judge our position and fuel was down to fifty percent. I glanced at the children in the back seat and my wife beside me.

Activating my mike. I called Thunder Bay Tower, giving, make of aircraft and registration and declared an emergency. Silence – no response. I called a second time then a third with no response. Switching my radio frequency to 121.5 I called again, "Any aircraft, May Day, May Day, May Day. This is Piper Tri Pacer JMF, May Day, May Day, Silence! I called again; May Day May Day May Day. This is Piper Tri Pacer JMF. Then response: Aircraft in distress, this is Air Canada 1207, Go Ahead. "Air Canada 1207 This is Piper Tri Pacer JMF, I am enroute to Thunder Bay, lost in the storm basic instruments and low on fuel. I need radar directions to the airport. Thunder Bay is not responding." "Pacer JMF stand by." The next couple of minutes seemed an eternity. "Pacer JMF this is Thunder Bay Tower, we have you on radar. New heading, maintain 278 degrees." Then, thankyou Lord a welcome sound; Tri pacer JMF, this is Thunder Bay, new heading 270 degrees." Pressing my mike I responded; "Thunder Bay tower, I am critically low on fuel can you approximate my remaining flying time?" "Tri Pacer JMF At your present heading and ground speed, 112 MPH, you are seventeen minutes from touchdown." "Thunder Bay, my right tank shows empty the left just about to hit empty as well. Your heading would take us over the city, I can't risk it. I have you in sight. I see a tanker half way across the bay, if we lose power I'll glide close to him maybe he can pick us up." "Pacer JMF, roger."

Number of souls on board?" "Two adults, two children."
As I began our descent, both gauges were reading empty. As
Elaine continued in her prayer, I focussed upon the runway.
It is close, closer, THEN under us.

Thank You, Lord, for seeing us through. As I taxied up
to the fuel tanks. "Lord, you truly were with us all the way".
The attendant, aware of our situation called out; "Who
was the last to fuel your tanks?" Your fuel caps were on
backwards and acted as a syphon. With these head winds,
you were lucky to make it in. Someone was looking after
you." I assured him SOMEONE was looking after us. I love
You Lord - Ron

Final Exam

Dear Jesus:

I anxiously await the results of my final exam. Will I have met the requirements for my master's degree? That final exam last Thursday afternoon, seemed to be light, but was it so? Thank you for the wisdom I have read in my pastor's handbook, noting especially the four cautions:

Time - The pastoral care needs are always greater than the time available to meet those needs

Expectations - It doesn't take a new pastor long to discover you can't meet all the expectations of your day.

Emotional fatigue - Pastors see a lot of emotional, mental, and spiritual needs

The Fix-it Syndrome - Many pastors are fixers by nature and personality. But many needing pastoral care, defy fixing, at least in the short term.

As a consequence we pastors feel frustrated and hopeless.

Seeing the mailman's arrival, with some hesitancy, I made my way out to our mailbox. An advertisement from

Canadian Tire, then a letter from the university! My hands were trembling (just a bit Lord) as I opened the letter. The word "congratulations" said I read! Thank you.

I Love You Lord Jesus - Ron

Loaves & Fishes

Dear Jesus

Thank You for our blessed miracle of the loaves and fishes. Six weeks had come and gone without a pay cheque from our church office. I remember looking for something for breakfast the cupboards were completely bare. Seven children expecting gifts under the tree and we had nothing to offer. I remember sitting in my office weeping when the telephone rang. It was Elaine calling me home. WHAT A SIGHT! Bags of flour, sugar, potatoes, a HUGE turkey, a mountain of canned goods. A Christmas cake, gifts for all the children. Even gifts for the two of us. Not to one soul had we shared our need! NOT ONE PERSON! Yet, God heard our prayers. He touched the hearts of our Christian brothers and sisters. Strangers became the hands of Jesus meeting our need.

O Lord, Church attendance was so vital to our wellbeing. We arrive here each Sunday morning to worship our Lord. We are family, the family of God! We also come to this holy place to love and support and pray for each other. Words from a hymn writer touched my thoughts:

We are one in the Spirit; we are one in the Lord.
We are one in the Spirit, we are one in the Lord
And we pray that all unity may one day be restored
And they'll know we are Christians by our love,
They will know we are Christians by our love.

I love You Lord – Ron

Do You Want To
Go To Hell

Dear Jesus

I recalled a most memorable Sunday morning when our family prepared to go to a new church. As I would be unemployed for a brief while we decided to attend a near-by little country church. We watched and listened with apprehension as the Sunday School superintendent began the session for the four children in attendance. Picking up a toddler, he raised the child over his head, then shaking the trembling tot, cried out; "Do you want to go to hell? Do you want to go to hell?" In panic the child screamed. Setting the child to the floor, he raised his hands upward calling out; "Praise the Lord, another child saved from the fires of Hell." Then he waved at an elderly grey-haired lady sitting in the front row. "Brothers and sisters, let us welcome sister Amelia who has offered to open God's word to us." Smiling, clapping her hands, Amelia screamed out HALLELUJAS! After a few sentences, she started 'dancing'.

On her way to the front 'danced out of her under-garments, then collided with the stove, knocking the pipes to the floor. I glanced at Elaine and her nod, a sign of agreement that we were not meant to be here. Quietly we made our way out of the building.

I Love You Lord – Ron

'Captain David'

Dear Jesus

I had promised our son David that for his fourth birthday, I'd take him with me in the airplane. That morning, he reminded me of my promise. Just after lunch we taxied out from the dock and took off, climbing into the clear blue sky. For the next several minutes, we enjoyed the flight. David was fascinated with the float planes I flew, declaring multiple times that he was going to be a pilot. I levelled off at 5000 feet. The air was still. "Davey, want to fly?" I motioned to the wheel, grinning he latched on exclaiming; "I'm a pilot", What I'd failed to notice was David's reaching down and turning a handle; the handle to our fuel flow. A few minutes passed when I heard a "deafening roar"; A deafening roar is often used by pilots to describe the sound of the stillness when their plane's engine stops. The silence was indeed deafening.

As my attempts at engine restart failed, and only trees below, I fought to keep calm. There just wasn't any place to land and we had only minutes remaining. Would we come out okay?" No place to set down" Could I settle into the trees? Then, I remembered on an earlier flight seeing a small lake off beyond that row of hills. At 2000 feet the lake came into view. As the floats touched the lakes surface, I called out in absolute sincerity; "Thank you Jesus."

I Love You Lord – Ron

Blessed Memories

Dear Jesus:

Today a letter from Division. Without warning we were ordered west to Hazelton British Columbia.

Hazelton was a time of blessing and, growth. It was a time when God strengthened us in preparation for our coming trial by fire. Hazleton was to be our shortest stay but most trying. It was a blessing that we couldn't see into the future. The scenery was beautiful, the people friendly and, God richly blessed our ministry. Yet a time of heavy stress. January to May had brought Dennis's broken ankle, David our eldest son's days in a coma from a burst appendix. Our second son's broken arm, the explosion and fire destroying our home and everything we owned. The brakes failing on our car and I jumped just as it plunged down the mountain.

Elaine's sister wrote; "I know you are trying to live a good life but must you take Job as your example?" Yet, this was the setting of God's greatest miracle in our lives. Our second son was diagnosed with leukaemia. Finally, we were told that he had less than three months to live. Our son who was given less than three months to live later would complete a term with Canadian Forces as an airborne specialist. He married a wonderful Christian partner; their three daughters are our pride and joy.

I Love You Lord – Ron

Called to Missions

Dear Jesus

Thinking back to those trying times of testing, perhaps I had the freedom to under- stand Job. Perhaps I could relate to him.

As we served You, our Lord, over the years, my prayer had always been: I'll go wherever You direct Lord, but PLEASE, not Saskatchewan. Please Lord not the bald prairies. Well wouldn't you know it! We were next appointed to North Battleford. Elaine wondered if it might have helped if we had prayed, "Please Lord, send us anywhere but Hawaii would be great!"' I doubt Lord if You would buy that approach. But we were content; we had at that time come the full circle. I remember how exhausted we were. Yet through the mental 'fog', we felt a calling to missions. Upon contacting a director of foreign missions, we were met with enthusiasm. The Hospital director at their mission in Papa New Guinea had resigned due to illness. They were relying on short term temps but where desperate to find a permanent placement. The position could be filled by either a medical doctor or a registered nurse. Elaine and I brought this as a prayer request before friends and family. With affirmation that this venture seemed to be within our Lord's will, I enrolled in the nursing program at Wascana College. Now we await our future.

I Love You Lord – Ron

Seeing Us Through

Dear Jesus

My first year went well, then into the second month of my final year – disaster. Guerrillas had burst into the mission station, executing all thirty of the staff. The hospital would remain closed indefinitely. After the prayers of family and friends, I felt Your leading to leave the nursing program.

It was sometime later that we thought we had lost our Lara. We were not home when she slipped away from her babysitter's grasp and ran out into the path of an oncoming truck. The doctor urged us to get to the hospital as quickly as we could. As we sat in the back of the taxi, I remember taking Elaine's hand "Honey we don't know, God may take her home or, He may leave her with us. But whatever happens He will see us through. He's with us all the way. Again, Lord, You blessed us with a happy ending.

Lara quickly regained her sight. It was a miracle that she came through her ordeal. But that was not the biggest miracle of all. The biggest miracle of all was that we who love the Lord are not promised a mountain-top existence. We are not spared from walking through deep, dark valleys, for they can come at any time in our walk. But, we are assured that whatever comes if we stay closely at His side, He will see us through.

I Love You Lord – Ron

Osteo-Arthritis

Dear Jesus

All is well we are enjoying a secure salary. Active in our church, teaching Sunday School, guest preaching, yet we KNEW we weren't in Your will. You wanted us to return to full time service. We hesitated; we weren't ready! Then our Heavenly Father moved. Closing the door on my employment. As I developed osteo-arthritis.

The day came when I had to retire and accept a disability pension. Days when I wanted to be up and about, were days when Elaine frequently had to help me dress. Such was my life, a dramatic change from the activities, and hobbies that I enjoyed. I was at 'home' in SCUBA gear on the bottom of the great lakes. I enjoyed the challenge of climbing the Rockies and the thrill of parachuting. For years we toured throughout Canada and the States on our Motorcycle.

First my hands lost their grip. My legs no longer carried my weight. Eventually, the doctor found a delicate balance between fogging my brain with drugs and keeping me functioning. This disability paved the way for me to enter seminary. Dear Jesus please give me enough courage to meet the challenge to further prepare for our calling as pastors.

Lord -this pain is getting to be more than I can bear. Please Lord, give me strength.

I Love You Lord - Ron

Total Peace

Dear Jesus

Then came the day Lord that You chose to change our lives forever. Throughout that night, I slept little as medication was not masking my pain. Unable to sleep, well before sunrise I hobbled out to the lake taking my hurt to You Lord. THEN, suddenly, as though time stood still. I seemed to be in a vacuum. There was no sound. A breath of warm comforting air brushed against me. I experienced total peace! Did it last minutes, seconds or a flash of time, I don't know. Just as suddenly, it was gone. The cool wind again blew into my face. Somewhere along the way I realized I was pain-free. God released me from my dark valley that I might better serve Him. Throughout our lives we have been thrust into many valleys. But each step of the way we have learned to reach out to You Lord in prayer: Prayers of thanksgiving for our daily bread, prayers of praise when all was not as we wished. And always we have learned the key words must be; nevertheless, not my will but Yours, and always You have honoured us.

You have ALWAYS answered our prayers. Not always in the way we wished. Sometimes the answer has been YES. Sometimes the answer has been - NO. Sometimes the answer has been – WAIT Always the answer has been a blessed one.

I Love You Lord – Ron

Difficult Paths

Dear Jesus

As we consider tomorrow's meeting, we sense a feeling of unrest, a sense tomorrow's path leads toward opposition to Your will.

To those special people around us, we respond; Should in God's time you be sent to new adventures in your faith. If you are called to walk a difficult path, you can be assured if you are faithful there will be only one set of footprints behind you in the sand for He will be carrying you. Perhaps the best of all advice comes from King Solomon; Proverbs 3:5 niv

> *Trust in the Lord with all your heart and*
> *Lean not on your own understanding.*

As we saw the corruption mount within the denomination we served, we were at a 'crossroads'. With much prayer we submitted our resignations. Heavenly Father, may our prayer together, with the words of our closing hymn prepare us and equip us all for our days ahead.

It may not be on the mountain's height,
Or over the stormy sea; It may not be at the
battle's front my Lord will have need of me;
But if by a still, small voice He calls to paths
I do not know, I'll go where You want me to
go, dear Lord, O'er mountain, or plain, or
sea; I'll say what You want me to say, dear
Lord, I'll be what You want me to be

I Love You Lord – Ron

A Tarnished Image

Dear Jesus:

It was time for our debriefing. A meeting with the divisional commander to finalize our resignation. As the meeting began, I sensed a tenseness in the air.

As our file was reviewed. It was asserted that I had never sent a letter of resignation. I gave assurance that I had done so. The officer quite emphatically insisted that I was mistaken and untruthful. When I said I could produce a` copy, the reply; for me to do so, I would have to write it. With the firm assertion that I was lying, the officer determined that to assure the church's best interests were met, one hundred dollars would be deducted from our car allowance.

Thinking of past transgressions and conduct of the Army, of thefts of church property and money, I feel it is time for our separation from a work with a phenomenal sacred history. Yet in this immediate area a tarnished image.

Turning to the Divisional Commander, with tears in my eyes I offered thanks for his clarifying which path I was to take. While I would not reveal the Army's ethics to the media, I was certain that the future would call the Army's general to order a complete house-cleaning of staff in the western provinces. With that we parted company without the customary handshake. Lord as always, the future is in Your hands.

I love You Lord – Ron

Que Sera, Sera

Dear Jesus

Upon search of Holy Writ, I see no words that dictate the following writing is contradictory to the theme of God's Word and Presence. However, as I follow news casts from around the world and in my neighbourhood, I am overwhelmed by the stench of sin that oozes from our environment and the general conduct of our people. Enter with me now into the possible realm of the Holy Creator:

No one but the King of Kings knows what the future holds. Therefore, based upon my understanding of Holy Writ, I choose to share with you what the future MAY hold. I am aware that some will find fault with my approach to our Lord's return however At the very least should my approach cause a renewed searching of the scriptures in that I rejoice. Que Sera, Sera Whatever will be will be.

Leaving the hospital following a visitation of a church member who was passionately devoted to our Lord and, shortly on her way to be with Him throughout eternity, I ran through the heavy rain to my car. My busy day was about to end at the hands of an intoxicated driver. Staggering from the bar, he crawled behind the wheel, and headed north into heavy rain on a south bound lane. Suddenly - something! – a shadow - a thunderous bang. One moment I was enjoying a refreshing rain, the next, hanging inverted by my seat belt. The smell of gasoline, a sudden glow, a roar of flames, burning pain, - then, I was enveloped in merciful relief and darkness. "WHERE AM I?" A VOICE: "**YOU ARE AT GLORY'S GATE**. This is your time for you to face your judgement. Your time to stand before the Cross and feel the same pain your Saviour felt for each transgression you committed from the day of your Salvation until this moment. A being of light stood beside me. "Who – what are you?" "I am the angel who is assigned to guide you to the Cross for your judgement. Now, before your own final judgement, it is time for you to observe that your family and friends have gathered for your funeral. The pastor is about to read the letter you wrote for this moment.

Listen as the pastor reads:" The pastor reached into his suit jacket and withdrew a letter. Pausing the pastor looked at the letter, the family and congregation. Slowly he opened the letter. Turning toward the family he informed; "I have been a pastor for many years, yet this is the first time I have had such a request. The words I now read are not my own, rather an urgent message, – No, more than that, a plea from our deceased brother. Let me say that I have spent much time in prayer as I considered the magnitude of these words. Placing the letter on the pulpit, the pastor begins to read.

Ron Hobden

To my beloved family:

Prior to taking my leave from among you, I felt a need to have the pastor pass on these few words at your gathering for my funeral. The time of our reunion, may be decades into the future, while here in Glory, twill be in the twinkle of the eye. I am blessed that these thoughts are directed to an exceptionally small number of my family. For as I sojourned with you, how blessedly exciting it was to see that close to one hundred percent of my loved ones enjoyed a personal relationship with the Lord and Savior. Thus said, these words from my heart reach out to the miniscule number of my beloved family who MAY remain uncommitted to the Savior. Only the almighty power of God can open one's eyes to see what is blindingly obvious. To miss the Savior's call is akin to the deaf being played Beethoven and Mozart and unsurprisingly being unimpressed. Like blind people being shown the Mona Lisa and likewise unsurprisingly being unimpressed. I joyously await the moment of the angel escorting you through the Gate first into the presence of the King, then, our reunion. Here within the Gate as one cannot experience pain, I shall be unaware of any of our family who in refusing a relationship with the Savior are escorted from Judgement into the eternal presence of the Prince of Darkness. May the faith of the many win over the hearts of the few.

Your letter ends with this plea; "My beloved Children, grandchildren, great-grand-children, siblings, as you hear these words know that I am experiencing the wonders of Glory. Now I await the moment when I shall meet you; when you shall meet your family who have come before you. Know that should there be even one of you who fails to accept King Jesus as personal Saviour, such a meeting shall never happen." May you who love the Saviour, through His guidance, introduce those in the family that are presently without the Saviour's touch.

Until we meet again;

Husband, Father, Grandfather,
Great Grandfather Ron

My guardian spoke up; You have great concerns that you may never see certain family members again. Now LOOK, look upon the Saviour's face; There is a smile. Because of your prayers and this moment of your funeral, some will turn to Him. But note; a look of pain, a tear trickles down His face. Some may ignore your plea for them to cry out to the Saviour. Their passage through the Gate may never take place. As the pastor has read your letter, may there be understanding. Let there be a cry "FORGIVE ME LORD,

Here at the cross one sees how great the Father values His holiness. He cannot violate that holiness even in order to save the lost. Here, we see wrath and mercy meet in glorious fulfilment – Some will be lost for they reside in a country where according to a recent poll, 76% classify themselves as 'religious', 53% believe there is a heaven. While only 27% believe hell exists.

"COME" my guardian directed. "It is your time to stand before the King in judgement." There at the Cross, I asked Jesus to come afresh into my heart, Then before me: followed every negative but now called what they were, every 'sin' I wilfully committed against the love of my Saviour. As each breach of holiness was exposed and the list beyond my imagination, I saw my Lord wreathe in agony, then a transferal to my soul of the pain my Saviour endured toward my forgiveness. "WHY oh Lord WHY". "My son it was the price I paid that you might pass through the Gate." For hours of earth time, yet a portion of a mil-second in Glory, I experienced my Saviour's suffering on my behalf. Then a silence, the time of my judgement. A VOICE, the voice determining my eternal future. "Well done my good and faithful servant, your angelic guide shall bring you before my throne". With a praise of Glory, my guardian motioned and together, we passed through the Gate into the presence of the King.

I mused. Did the prophet Isaiah put it all in perspective as he wrote? See the Lord in his splendour. This is what the LORD says: "Heaven is my throne, and the earth is my footstool. Could you build me a temple as good as that? Could you build me such a resting place? My hands have made both heaven and earth; they and everything in them are mine. I, the LORD, have spoken! I will bless those who have humble and contrite hearts, who tremble at my word". (Isaiah 66:1–2 NLT)

Ever from our understanding of the eternal, let us be struck by the glory of the Lord. Let us understand what He asks of his people since He is the Almighty God. Now at this moment I understood that while in our earthly body He demands our all. From us, a yielding heart that trembles at the very words of God and desires to obey. Even now, with eyes adjusted to Glory's realm I knew that there were no words, no illustrations that could even come close to a description of what was before me. As my mind was now 'upgraded' from human standard to 'Glory standard', I was able to grasp the concept of time. Now I understood 2 Peter 3:8, KJV:

> But, beloved, be not ignorant of this one thing, that one day is with the Lord as a thousand years, and a thousand years as one day.

I was now provided with the eternal knowledge that time was 'fluid'. Ones judgement before the Cross could involve hours, days, weeks of earth time yet a fleeting millisecond here in Glory. My angel added a note of clarity to my ever-increasing awareness of the greatness before me, Paul would centuries later provide the only two options available to the humans created in the garden

Option ONE by St. Matthew: Two Pathways—One Leading To Life "Enter through the narrow gate, because the gate is wide and the way is spacious that leads to destruction, and there are many who enter through it. But the gate is narrow and the way is difficult that leads to life, and there are few who find it. Matthew 7:13-14

Option TWO by St. Paul: "For the wages of sin is death, but the gift of God is eternal life in Christ Jesus our Lord" Romans 6:23

With my affirmation, my guide continued; "Now, to consider the Great Gulf, I must take you back to Isaiah 26. See how the prophet signifies the difference in moral character between the uncommitted and the committed as we see the destiny of the wealthy man and the poor Lazarus. The fixing of the gulf means that after death, the character of a person cannot be altered. It is too late to change. This gap, this gulf of separation striped away the rich man by his own volition, an eternal separation from the eternal happiness of "Abraham's bosom". Yet the profound happiness rewarded to the beggar, his acceptance of a personal Lord and Saviour provided for him to be carried by the angels to

"But, I queried, can mankind, no matter how worthy, ever really fathom the holiness of God?

Is it not impossible for creatures of imperfection to obey His command to, "Be holy, because I am holy" as in 1 Peter 1:15–16? How can anyone set themselves totally apart from sin? My guardians response was enlightening; "You now have clarity of thought. Now you understand, that at the time of the beginning, God intended for His creation to understand, to experience His glory. Adam's descendants were the culmination of God's creative activity. Human existence was not a random accident. God knew who and what He was creating, and He intended for each one of us to be eligible to choose or to reject the holiness of eternity, that the divine gift of everlasting holiness was by choice. The message first by the prophets, then by the Lamb and as reminder to the human psyche, the sending forth of pastors, to convey the great theme of God's holy Word.

> *"All must all appear before the judgment seat of Christ, so that each of us may receive what is due us for the things done while in the body, whether good or bad"*. 2 Corinthians.5:10

> *For the law is made not for the righteous but for lawbreakers and rebels, the ungodly*

and sinful, the unholy, the irreligious; for murderers, for the sexually immoral, for that practicing homo-sexual for liars and perjurers—and for whatever else is contrary to the sound doctrine." 1Timothy 1:9-10

I now recalled that as I appeared before the cross to face my judgement. There were some before me. First, a woman, perhaps in her early forties, yet badly scarred. Scarred by some object that caused her demise. The second, a man of mid-life years. My gaze now fixed upon the woman as she fell before the Cross. My guardian now clarified, 'She is about to see her life unfold; As a teen she reached out to Jesus pledging a personal relationship. Clearly, she saw her parent's tears when she began dating a college classmate. Their dismay when she informed them that she had accepted his proposal of marriage.

For the first few months, they lived as newly weds. Then unreasonable demands, fits of anger, shouting, shoving, then with the birth of their two children, her responsibilities as mother to their daily needs, became seen as ignoring her mate. Anger! Anger, rage a husband's scream of anger, a sharp pain as a hammer struck the side of her head, darkness. Then before her, a Cross and a shining gate. Her judgement proceeded to conclusion, now her guide led her to the gate. "Lee", you are at the beginning of forever. You have been judged. You have heard your Saviour's verdict. His word; "Well done, good and faithful servant". In a moment I shall guide you through the gate. On this side, you remember all the negative and positive moments of your life from the instant you accepted Christ as Saviour until this moment following your judgement. Once through the Gate you will have entered into your Saviour's presence. A place where all the hurts of your past life are forever removed. As your spirit guide, I will answer your first questions and your wonder. But, now, your Saviour, King Jesus is calling you to Him".

My thoughts harmonized with Lee's as I witnessed her thought patterns. when she received her initial welcome from her Lord. She was enabled in an instant, to understand that countless events could happen almost simultaneously, yet be experienced as individual moments, hours, days even months. Now with the conclusion of her judgement, for the first time in many earth years an intense peace and joy filled her soul. She was now a judged, examined, forgiven resident of Glory, relieved of every memory of past suffering.

Lights, took shape around her. Strange at first to her, then, while foreign in appearance, they were recognizable smiling entities. Her grandmother, a childhood friend she hadn't seen for many years. Friends from the church she'd attended before her husband forced her to leave. "Before you meet your welcoming committee, I

I see a look of surprise. While you suspected that Heaven's inhabitants would be 'ghostlike", they are solid forms, different from their earthly bodies, yet you recognize each one and know every positive role they played for the Kingdom while in their earthly bodies, as we saw you standing before the cross. Auntie is here waiting to welcome you. First, recall the words of the prophet Jeremiah:

> *For I know the plans I have for you" this is the LORD's declaration—" plans for your well-being, not for disaster, to give you a future*

and a hope. I will bless you with a future
filled with hope—a future of success, not of
suffering. Jer.29:11.

"Here is your future. Here is your hope. here you are forever beyond hurt, pain and loneliness. Meet your welcoming committee, they have much to share. Then, see the elders gathering around the throne, the angelic choir, a beckoning Jesus. This is Glory, now go into the arms of Jesus. Motioning, her guardian ushered Helen through the open Gate and before the Throne. If only I had the ability to describe the sights, the sounds, the continual excitement of joy as one is permitted the positives the joys of those who have passed through judgement. Only the King could fashion an existence where within the Gate the positives, the blessed moments the surrender of one's entirety to the King.

My guardian's thoughts touched my soul; "It is permitted for you to pass through the gate for a Glory moment to witness specific judgements. This is very surprising to me, yet there is never a question of assignments from the throne. Before you the Cross for souls in judgement. There before me a little girl, perhaps twelve years of age and a cluster of adult men and women. The child was uncontrollably sobbing. "Why is she crying", one in the cluster asked. From the Cross a response; "She is crying because in this moment of her trial before Judgement is her memory of your encounter. She is the child that you forbid the wearing of a Tee shirt in your classroom. There she stands before the Cross in her judgement, look again" displayed upon her Tee shirt the words 'Jesus Loves Me'. came the voice of Judgement REMEMBER You were the one who directed that child's Tee shirt be removed and taken from her. Feel the pain you caused the child." Time passed as this innocent little one turned her heart and soul over to Jesus transferring her sorrow into a joyful teen, a faithful wife and mother to the moment when tragedy ruled. The little one, a member of your class, Now a resident of Glory." Do you not recall these My words;" *"If anyone causes one of these little ones, those who believe in me to stumble, it would be better for them to have a large mill- stone hung around their neck and to be drowned in the depths of the sea." NOW, depart from Me, I never knew you."* Matthew 18:6

Beside him the angel who would lead him to meet the Satanic horde motioned. Then I recalled Luke's insertion of chapter 16:

> *The rich man also died and was buried. In Hades, where he was in torment, he looked up and saw Abraham far away, with Lazarus by his side. So he called to him, 'Father Abraham, have pity on me and send Lazarus to dip the tip of his finger in water and cool my tongue, because I am in agony in this fire.'*
> *"But Abraham replied, 'Son, remember that in your lifetime you received your good things, while Lazarus received bad things, but now he is comforted here and you are in agony. And besides all this, between us and you a great chasm has been set in place, so that those who want to go from here to you cannot, nor can anyone cross over from there to us.'*

Luke 16:22 – 26

Before The Cross

Again, my guardian's thoughts filled my consciousness. "As God was intimately involved in your life, so He is, in every life of His committed. The decisions He made, decisions about you daily, decisions to do with answers to your prayers, bestowing His blessings on you, protecting you and even allowing you to endure trials are for all His children." Standing before the throne I heard the angelic host sing;

> *"Oh Lord our God your glory is your excellence*
> *excellence that calls for our praise. Your glory*
> *is your brilliance over all others. Your great-*
> *ness of power which calls out our fear and*
> *honour."*

An angel paused, then nodded; "I am to accompany a soul through judgement;" As I step through the Gate, I shall receive a complete life 'story' of the one standing before the cross. This will parallel an entry in your diary years ago when, as a stressed pastor, you brought one of your contacts before the Lord: So many times, he had 'heard' the words of peace and love and promise of King Jesus. Now, one by one, every opportunity he's had to evaluate his position with the Saviour. The message of every funeral he'd attended, every wedding, every Christmas Eve Service, a multitude of television evangelists now etched in the depths of his memory and his response to each opportunity clearly played out before him. Now, he is called to judgement. In anger, he had turned away, refuting any suggestion of forgiveness. Ignoring the warnings of the Holy Word such as: *"All must all appear before the judgment seat of Christ, so that each of us may receive what is due us for the things done while in the body, whether good or bad"*. Cor. 5:10. Now to him, "Depart from Me I never knew you." William Booth the Salvation Army founder's concern for our present generation expressed his fear as he related: "I consider that the chief dangers which confront the coming century will be religion without the Holy Ghost, Christianity without Christ, forgiveness without repentance, salvation without regeneration, politics without God, and heaven without hell."

You are to accompany me beyond the gate". "Now witness divine judgment. Here tragedy unfolds"; A man with a gun walked down a hall, shooting one after another, until he was confronted and shot by police officers. Now, he stands in judgement. First, before him, is a teenager. He watches, as how history would have unfolded had he not so tragically ended the child's life. What could have been would never be. First, would have been this youth's dream, to complete high school, college, graduation with distinction. He was destined to became a para-medic, marry, two children, then would risk his life to save a child from a burning building. Years would have passed as that rescued child grew to become the scientist who discovered a new drug for ovarian cancer. I watched as the emotions, the pain of what could have been, was transferred to the man standing in judgement, as he endured the loneliness the anguish and broken dreams of each one whose life he had scarred. While this judgement took only a millisecond, outside the gate where he stood, his experience was in 'real earth time'. I recalled the words of Peter: *With the LORD a day is like a thousand years, and a thousand years are like a day. 2 Peter 3:8*

Upon conclusion, the voice of the King; "*In prison, you heard the Chaplin's message. You reached out to Me for forgiveness. Your plea for My forgiveness was genuine. Here before the Cross, my Judgement. Enter now into eternal peace. My faithful servant.*"

Here beyond the Gate, I questioned; How can this be? How can it be?" To which my angelic guide responded; "Yes, that man committed horrendous sin. But the Cross is empowered to bring to Glory even the vilest offender who from his heart pleads forgiveness. The pain that he suffered before the Cross for his evil, now forever forgotten. This newest saint assumes residence in Glory. As you, he is forever in the arms of Jesus." Consider the entries in your diary.

My guide explained; "Do you recall one evening shortly thereafter that you came across the words that clarified?" "It is appointed; that you shall now have your question answered: "Is this saying", I questioned; that people can make it by by 'the skin of their teeth' by repenting in their last dying breath?" Surely their degree of eternal contentment will not be nearly as great as that of those who have been serving Christ faithfully for many, years for decades?" and my guardian's reply. "The example of the thief on the cross is often cited as the precedent for deathbed conversions. And so have many who repent and confess Christ on their deathbeds. All judgement is from the King". A king so holy that the warning "...You cannot see my face, for no one may see me and live." Exodus 33:20, NIV. As the words of the prophet Moses touched my soul, I remembered the work of a hymnwriter; "When I see Jesus Amen When I see the man who died for me the one who set me free Amen All my troubles will be over When I see Jesus Amen." A smile and nod from the King was royal accent to once, that which was hidden.

O Lord – How I Love You - Ron

To Admire or Consume

As I wandered about the magnificence of Glory I considered, for what purpose – the great walls surrounding all of Glory? Sensing my pondering an angel approached. "You are confused by the immense walls. Recall John's theme from Revelation: Recall the pre-ordained war in Heaven at the end of the age. In this war, the archangel Michael and his angelic troops shall contend against Satan and his fallen angels. Lacking the strength and power to defend their territory, or to breach these walls, Satan and his evil horde shall be "hurled" to the earth and forever evicted from Heaven". As suddenly as he had arrived he was gone. Then as my pondering settled a movement before me; 'it's a shimmering at my right, A stranger that I in an instant recognized and of whom here in Glory had complete knowledge. Ibarashi! what a joy it was to meet one of Japan's greatest Christian heroes.

As a young teen in the 16th century, he was indicted with the criminal charge of being a Christian. He was urged to renounce his faith in Jesus, but chose the cross. Ibarashi interrupted my thinking; We have all eternity to enjoy each other's company. "I notice your affinity to your 'aunt Sarah'.

It is permitted for you to go back in time to the moment of the positives of her trial. You are permitted to stand beside her at her judgement as she is complimented by her Lord for her service. Here on this side of the Gate, no negative thoughts, events or questioning can ever filter into Glory.

Silently I stood before the Cross as Aunt Sarah's judgement proceeded. There, her life unfolded – laid bare from the moment she had accepted the Christ as personal Saviour. All the moments of blessed and sacred events of her life were portrayed. The times of joy she'd echoed into Glory. Then, the words of forever joy; The words of the King; 'Well done, good and faithful servant! You have been faithful in life, enter into the joy of your master."

My own joy multiplied a thousand times more as I listened to the angel choir proclaiming their Holy Praise of Aunt Sara's life and judgement there, upon the throne of God. And there, the Mercy Seat where God sat surrounded by legions of angels in Glory with power proclaiming and blessing. Suddenly, following her celebration at the Saviour's side, she was transported to the mansion the King had readied for her. Then after joining with the angelic choir before the throne, she appeared at my side. "Oh Ron, I recalled John's words in explanation of all this before us from Revelation 4:8-11.

Each of the four living creatures had six wings and was covered with eyes all around, even under its wings. Day and night they never stop saying: "'Holy, holy, holy is the Lord God Almighty,' who was, and is, and is to come."

"Ron, at this moment I remember how I watched you through your childhood, teens, marriage, children and finally, you're heeding your Lord's call into ministry. Money wasn't plentiful in your home, yet it was admirable how your parents persevered and imparted their wisdom to you and your siblings. I watched as you took your first steps toward the ministry of the Word and Sacrament. I recalled that one of your first Sundays the 11:00 a.m. service at Massey was well attended. At Nairn. for the 2:00 p.m. meeting there wasn't a car in the parking lot. The evening service at Walford was well attended and at the service's end, your mom and dad, were the last ones out the door, I knew that you would always remember and cherish your father's words; "Ron, we are very proud of you". I shall thank our Lord, for today and keep you in prayer through the summer. As you prepare for this challenge. Remember your Lord's advice through Timothy;

> *"Let no one despise you for your youth, but set*
> *the believers an example in speech, in conduct.*
> 1 Timothy 4:12

I glanced over your shoulder as you turned to your diary and penned the adventure of your first preaching duty: Never could at that moment

You imagine, even fantasize. Proclaiming God's Holy Word as you stood behind pulpits in The United States, England, Scotland, Japan and in your homeland. I am being called, we have all of eternity to focus our thoughts upon our service"

Golly in Glory

As a figure appeared at my side, I knew instantly it was Ibaraki. "Ron," he said, "I note that your thought harbours upon Golly. You question, could Golly be here? First let us join the choir of the Seraphim. The moment was Heavenly, glorious! Before us the six-winged angelicas, those closest to God, lifting their voices in continual praise, glorifying the Father by calling out, "Holy, Holy, Holy is the Lord God of Hosts. After the praise ended, Ibaraki approached; "I see that you are still wondering about Golly; You are questioning, do animals pass through the Gate? Let the words of Isaiah flow through your thought as you recall the prophet's wisdom:"

> *"The wolf also shall dwell with the lamb,*
> *The leopard shall lie down with the young*
> *goat, the calf and the young lion and the*
> *fatling together; And a little child shall lead*
> *them. The cow and the bear shall graze;*
> *Their young ones shall lie down together;*
>
> *And the lion shall eat straw like the ox.*
> *The nursing child shall play by the cobra's hole,*

And the weaned child shall put his hand in the viper's den. They shall not hurt nor destroy in all My holy mountain, For the earth shall be full of the knowledge of the LORD. As the waters cover the sea".

Isaiah 11:6-9 NIV

The angelic being at my side suggested that perhaps I should turn to the wisdom of Holy Writ. Of Acts 3:21, Romans 8:18–22, Isaiah 11:6– 8, Isaiah 65:17 and Revelation 21:1.

It is not for me to enlighten you, but I have been granted the ability to have you for a moment feel how Golly's presence would be, should he be here; Now, for an instant - enjoy:" I felt a loving touch. It was Golly! Golly the St. Bernard who had been my greatest childhood treasure. When we children were not yet mature enough to sense danger, so many times, Golly had stood between us and a threat whatever it might be. It was said that there was not a mean bone in Golly's body. Yet during the few times that neighbouring kids became aggressive in play, Golly's low-pitched growl was all that it took. Thank you, Lord, for this moment. During my pastoral years, the question of pets making it to Glory was seldom, if ever, brought up. An angelic voice broke the silence as he appeared at my side. *"Your Golly was truly blessed to have a secure home, yet in so many cases he was an exception to the rule. Once again you are permitted to observe judgement". Animal cruelty can often be difficult to recognize but it has proven to be a pervasive problem. No species or community is exempt from the experience of animal abuse and neglect. Here are but a few trials and judgements".*

The Holy City

On one of my countless traverses of the eternal city with mother and dad, brother Ray and sister Fran, we recalled the various biblical descriptions of this realm of Glory; It was upon my arrival that my spirit introducer cautioned I must not suppose the heavenly Jerusalem to be in reality adorned with gold and precious stones, for that was the mode of expression human minds could understand. The heavenly city was as much superior to earth as gold is to dirt, as pearls to common stone, the stars to candles, the sun to a torch, and mortal architects to God, the immortal Creator of all things as recorded in Holy Writ,

As we wandered about, Granny Hobden gazing at all the wonders before us commented: "Whenever people attempted to imagine heaven, they sometimes pictured ethereal images like angels loafing on clouds or chubby cherubs strumming on harps. But maintaining this perspective was so difficult when bombarded with numerous misconceptions about heaven in popular cultures. There were usually three of the most common ideas about heaven.

First: Heaven is where good people will spend eternity. They failed to take into their souls, when scriptures spoke clearly that there is no one who is good enough for heaven that any righteousness we think we had is like a "filthy rag" when held up to the standard of Gods holiness.

Second: those who thought they were good enough for heaven. How self-deceived - their pride separated them from God who "opposes the proud but gives grace to the humble" If only they had taken James words to heart *"God opposes the proud but shows favour to the humble."* James 4:6.

Third the multitude of bewildered souls whose self image refuses to consider Matthew's warning, his cautioning explanation that our Lord proclaimed in Matthew 7:14 that the way to heaven is small and narrow, and "only a few find it" Yet, the terrifying truth of the matter is that one of the scariest warnings Jesus ever gave was about people who will be self-deceived. They will think they are following Christ and many of them will even be doing miracles in his name, but they will not be allowed entrance to heaven. At the end of their earthly lives, Jesus will reveal to them that he never knew them. Upon ones passing through the Gate the mystery unfolds to the greatest of truths that our tree of life is Jesus Christ, granting us immortality through His defeat of death on the cross. Because of the ancestral sin of Adam and Eve, we now have the knowledge of good and evil and the free will to choose between the life-giving Christ or the deadly pursuit of selfish passion. Again, Ken appeared at our side. Smiling Ken turned to my mother; "Mary, I always admired your knack of what I call; "Loving Deception". Surely Jesus had touched your heart enabling you to provide for your family a feast out of the mundane. When the cupboard was bare, you provided a feast! A family treat just had to be sage balls. How your children loved those sage balls. It wasn't until they were all grown, with families of their own. That you let the 'cat' out of the bag." Whenever your pantry was bare, you inevitably asked, 'any ideas for supper', to which there was always, "Could we have sage balls." You mashed a few potatoes, added a generous amount of spices and a healthy coating of sage, then into the oven as the kids watched in anticipation."

Dad interjected: "The King is calling us." As mother and father took their leave, appearing at my side, Elaine's mother with invitation to her mansion: In less than an instant we arrived.' She looked at me for a moment, "Ron, I still stand amazed at, what we used to call - time.' Do you realize that the distance we just travelled in less than a blink of an eye was farther than the four miles that you walked with your father, from the farm to Massey, so you could take in a Saturday afternoon movie? Further than the fourteen kilometres that you peddled your bicycle to visit my daughter?"

She paused for a moment then; uttered "An angel, I'm being summoned to the throne", and she was gone. GONE but yet as all residents of Glory, she was only a fraction of an earth second away. An entity appeared; "as this is Glory, I already know we have something in common.

For due to a drunken driver, He too walked through the Gate." Now excuse me I'm off to join the choir. And he was gone, but, I'd see him again, often.

Thank you, Jesus, I whispered and, I saw my King's smile. "My child every soul that through you was assisted in their journey are awaiting to meet and to rejoice with you. They are all just a thought away." "But Lord what about those whose personality whose conduct rejected You?" "Do not dwell upon those were sentenced to an eternity without hope. However, I will permit you to pass through the Gate for a brief moment to witness trials of accused that you may better comprehend the justice of their sentencing:

Stepping through the Gate I Noticed two couples before the Cross: each subscribed to the urging of an angel of Satan. Breaking a sacred law of 'Love upon the earth'

First in Holy Writ, first Corinthians 6, *"Men who practice homosexuality, shall not inherit the kingdom of God.* Then in Romans 1:26-27, *Women who exchanged natural relations for those that are contrary to nature; receiving in themselves the due penalty for their error.* From this there is no reprieve. In their case both couples were church members. One of many churches that deleted texts from my holy Word. These days, demons are hard at work urging membership into these "nests of abomination."

The Flying Turtle

Dear Jesus

While enjoying my mansion I recalled certain inserts from my diary; My recording of an incident. Harvey, the school principal, suggested that the students might enjoy a Bible study.

At the Bible Book Store I found Herman The Flying Turtle, a 15-minute movie focusing upon Heavenly Angels. The movie had just nicely started when, a member of the school board entered the room. Seeing the movie, she gasped, ran up to the front and pulled the cord, shutting down the movie. Shaking her fist at me in anger, she blurted out. "Don't you know that movies are a tool of Satan? There will be none of that here." Years later I would learn that the church had a fanatical understanding of God's Holy Writ. An understanding that would have serious 'eternal consequences' for several attendees. One such case was her daughter having lived under the influence of such a deranged faith had fallen into the depths, as a street walker in Vancouver. From a tear that ran down the King's face I knew that she was not the only attendee that through this church was through its teaching, consigned to everlasting Hell.

Dear Lord, to those who subscribed to this teaching and still walking the earth? Will they be saved. Will the lady whom I mention repent?

M.A.P.S.

Dear Diary

Elaine and I were really enjoying the blessings we were experiencing from our stint with M.A.P.S., a volunteer organization for folks with RVs to park on the projects property and offer their skills to the project. At this time we were volunteering at a Boy's Ranch. Elaine was working in the office while I was working on the grounds.

Thankyou Lord for keeping the numerous gators and those large snakes at bay. News of our volunteering at the ranch was noticed by a Boy's Ranch up on the Pan Handle. They were in desperate need of teachers, would we 'please' come to them?" As we committed this to our Lord, we felt misgivings, yet put it down to an invite to work in an unknown field. Lord, help us in the future to be more attuned to Your voice.

Upon our arrival, we were given a 'crash course' in camp policy and their educational program. We were immediately introduced to our classes. As the boys were all wards of the court we were briefed on camp and legal requirements. The first week passed with only a few minor glitches. Then

Monday morning of the second week before class the director met with me and asked how things were going. After a few minutes of words of appreciation and praise for our work, he asked if I would take on one additional responsibility. "Would you lead our Wednesday morning chapels?" Upon my agreeing, he asked; "Do you speak in tongues"?

When I responded that, that was not one of my gifts. He thought for a moment then said, 'Okay you can get by, by just whispering "bow ties and dirty socks". This would be a mocking of the Holy Spirit, blasphemy! In shock we considered what we had gotten into as we included in our thoughts, teens reports that during their Wednesday evening prayer meeting they received rewards whenever they would dance around the church and shout out their version of "tongues". Within ninety minutes, our car was packed and we were headed north to Canada and home. As we drove we considered again the words of Holy Writ from Acts 2:4 NLT; And everyone present was filled with the Holy Spirit and began speaking in other languages, as the Holy Spirit gave them this ability. Therefore, there should never be a question of the validity of the Holy Spirit's gift of tongues. Yet, to falsely claim this gift was lying against the Holy Spirit which is blasphemy, and an example of a mental imbalance defined as obsessive-compulsive disorder. They are just as 'hooked' as a drug addict, and the more they use the fake language, the more they will do so, because when they stop, their minds compel them to continue.

Lord Jesus help us to listen more closely that we may recognize Your leading.

I love You Lord – Ron

Mistaken Identity

Dear Jesus:

My pilot's license was only a few months old. I took every opportunity to build up flying hours. This morning the weather was exceedingly friendly, A perfect time to add a couple of hours flying time in my log book. I topped off the fuel in the aircraft designated to me and went back into the hanger.

I heard the door opening as Bill and two passengers entered. Bill jotted his plane's registration on the board then headed out the door while I went back to my flight chart. After several moments, I heard their plane's engine turning over, then acceleration as the Cessna 180 gained speed. Glancing out the window, I saw it lift off. As I headed to my aircraft, I saw that Bill must have switched planes. Not a problem I'd take the one he'd signed out. As I began my pre-flight check I noticed that the tanks were nearly empty. Bill's lazy streak, had obviously caught up with him. After fuelling 'Bill's plane' – now mine, and finishing my prefight check, the engine came to life, after taxiing away from the dock I pulled back on the yolk and land fell below. Lord, as I levelled off at 5000 feet was this when Your inspiration came to play. For some 'unknow reason" I thought I'd add another three thousand feet. Lord, You knew what those three thousand feet would mean later in the flight. It was a beautiful sunny day with only a few small clouds floating endlessly by. Glancing at the engine heat gauge heading toward the red zone I put the craft into a steep bank heading back toward base. On my map, I noticed that there was a lake a few degrees to my right. I Issued an unanswered May Day call. The needle now fully in the red, I eased back on the throttle then within an easy gliding distance to the lake, I shut down the engine to be greeted by the unmistaken roar of silence. This time however – No Panic and the plane was soon safely secured to a tree.

After repeated unanswered calls, I switched the radio to the A.M. band to catch the 2:00 p.m. news before heading through the bush to highway 17, I calculated to be about 4 kilometres to the north. I had just unwrapped a sandwich when: "This is CKSO Sudbury with the afternoon news. We begin with a sad item. A light plane from Long Lake Aviation crashed into Twin Narrows Lake. Taking the life of the pilot, Ronald Hobden, the lone occupant. His family has been notified. Further update as available." Grabbing the mike, I called in desperation to the base then on 121.5, still no answer. A ninety minute dash through the bush then highway 17 was in sight.

My desperate waves attracted the fourth vehicle. As I started with my explanation, I noted the drivers confused look. He had been listening to the news. However, I was able to assure him I WAS Ron. Hobden. Somehow, they had mixed up the registrations on our aircraft. Bill must be dead! Believing my almost impossible story, the driver asked, "Okay, where do you want me to take you?" "My car is at Long Lake Base." Twenty minutes later, I called Elaine to find that she had just made it home from class and hadn't yet turned on the radio. Next, I called my parents; "Dad it's all a mistake, I'm alive and well." By this time family, aunts and uncles, neighbours had collected at the farm. At the sound of my voice, dad was finally convinced that it actually WAS my voice. As silence reigned, dad explained our phone call.

The next contact was to the Ontario Provincial Police. "Thankyou Mr. Hobden, please remain where you are, an officer will be with you shortly. "Upon the officer's arrival, my driver's license convinced him that my story was legit, I was The Ronald Hobden in the news and very much alive. Bill's family were notified, the news corrected. Later it was learned that as next-door neighbours were knocking at dad's door to express their condolences, they thought that the laughter and carryings on were the reaction of a family upon the death of their eldest son and was despicable. They left without contact. It would be a couple of days before dad learned of their confusion, and brought them up to date.

Dear Jesus how might I show Your love and care to Bill's grieving parents? Be with me at the funeral that I might share Your care.

I love You Lord – Ron

THE O.P.P.

Dear Jesus

The inspector sat across the desk and he asked; "Hobden want do you want in life?" "Sir," I replied "I want your job and I'm willing to work to get it." Three months later I was in Police College. Upon graduation, I was posted to Spanish, Ontario, a detachment patrol area that included Elaine's and my home area. I would be policing my home town, my relatives, friends, classmates. Lord, I feel your calling to preach the word, I cannot imagine how this fits together. At the same time, I somehow sensed that I was to apply to the Ontario Provincial Police. I can't see how this all fits together. Lord I'm going to need Your help here. There will be conflicts as I enforce regulations in my home community. How can conflict be an asset for any future ministry? I give all those questions to You. I give You my restlessness, my fears and worries. My dreams, and desires. My abilities and inabilities. Use me as You please. Close the wrong doors, open the right ones. Do all the miracles that need to be done on my behalf. Prepare me to do whatever you have planned for me to do. Lord, this morning I read the assurance of

Jeremiah as he advised that You were in charge. Opening my bible, I turned to Jeremiah 29:11

> *For I know the plans I have for you, declares the Lord, plans for welfare and not for evil, to give you a future and a hope.*

Little Detroit – Dive

Dear Jesus:

Last afternoon Cpl. Frank suggested it was time to bring our deep water diving up to speed. Let's make it 9:00 tomorrow morning. There's a lake vessel in just over one hundred and twenty feet. So it's straight down five minutes bottom time then a normal assent. So it was that arriving on site we were greeted by a clear sunny day. At 10:15 four of our team dropped over the vessel's side. As bottom loomed, I spotted the hulk. A glance at my watch showed that I had seven minutes to ascent. Time to do a swim pass of the lake freighter. Something was moving at the vessel's stern! Seemed to be loose rigging. It was time to head for surface. I signalled to my diving buddy I was ready to ascend. He nodded and began his ascent. Something caught my eye, As I reached down to the pile there was a shift in current trapping my arm. The harder I struggled the tighter the object upon my arm. A minute possibly two passed before I heard a distinctive 'ping'. My J valve activation signalled my tank was empty and that I had at most five minutes remaining in the J. valve I knew that struggle would delete my moments of remaining air. O Lord I cried, I'm in Your hands. A moment later the weight shifted. Dropping my weigh belt, I shot to surface bursting both ear drums on the accent. A small price to pay,

I Love You Lord – Ron

Transferred to
White River'

Dear Jesus

Two years have passed quickly. Then an abrupt change. Arriving at detachment this morning I was handed a letter. 'Transferred to White River'. Lord, what will this posting bring? With apprehension we prepared for the move. From our first Sunday we were accepted into the church fellowship. A warm and caring congregation. However, a warm and caring congregation, with a very ill minister and a shortage of staff! Soon, Elaine was Sunday School Superintendent and I was filling in behind the pulpit.

Within a few months our minister's heart gave out. Lord, did You plan this all along? Interesting, Lord, how things unravel when You are in charge! The Sargent suggested that as long as work at the church didn't conflict, I could take my lunch hour Sundays at church time. Thank you, Lord this is not just a job, it's my calling. May Holy Writ remind me of the importance of what I do. May I always be fair, strong and Not afraid of day to day challenges. For the

Ron Hobden

next year only once did I miss Sunday worship. There were times when I would arrive, to find that one of the elders had commenced the service, I would rush in, take off my Sam Brown and place it along with my service revolver under the pulpit and the service would proceed.

I Love You Lord – Ron

Constable Hobden

Dear Jesus

Lord, being a Police Officer in a small community is interesting work. Off duty I coach junior hockey and ball teams and involvement in the church. While on duty, because of the uniform some kept their distance while the majority showed their appreciation through waves and smiles. Lord, give me wisdom when dealing with those who come into conflict with the law. Somehow, for some reason the words of the prophet came into my mind; I thought of him standing at the entrance of his cave as it was revealed to him:

The Lord was not in the wind; and after the wind an earthquake, but the Lord was not. was not in the earth-quake; and after the earthquake a fire, but the Lord was not in the fire; and after the fire a still small voice. 1 Kings 19:11-12

As I questioned, I came across the words of an unknown theologian who penned; "This is, perhaps, the most forcible example of moral and spiritual teaching in a dramatic form in the whole range of Holy Scripture. And when it is regarded in the light of the mental condition of the prophet to whom it was granted, its force is still more evident. Elijah—the prophet of fire—a man of highly-strung emotional nature, a man who sometimes rose very high, but, like all such men, sometimes sank very low."

I love You Lord – Ron

My Pocket New Testament

Dear Jesus:

My work as a police officer was unique and above all interesting. I enjoyed highway patrol. Each season had its own challenges. One had to always be 'on their toes' during late spring – early summer, as moose accidents were of epidemic proportions. During one month, I had twenty-one collisions.

As the moose were extremely large animals sometimes weighing up to 723 Kg, it was all too common to investigate a fatality. Part of the investigation involved notifying the next of kin. This was always a challenge. As the season progressed, I was pressured more and more to be the officer who delivered the sad news. Finally I had reached what I thought was the end of my endurance. I knocked on the sergeant's door, entered and most upset countered; Sargent, I notified a family last evening and now I'm to knock on the door of a family whose daughter is deceased. I am getting more than my share of these fatalities." The sergeant motioned for me to shut the door. "Hobden, what's in your back pocket?" "My wallet sir". "Your other pocket". Reaching back, I held up my testament. "That's why I send you." I nodded and withdrew from the office. Jesus forgive me, may my presentation to those who mourn be sacred and filled with Your Love.

I love You Lord - Ron

JUMP

Dear Jesus:

I remember so well the morning as I crawled out of bed, my asking that You watch over me that day. That very evening, I answered a family plea for help. Upon arriving at the residence, I heard a scream for help from within. As I forced open the door, I 'felt' an urge (more like a command) to jump, I responded as bullet struck the door where I had been a second earlier. As this was a charge of attempted manslaughter the trial was scheduled to be held some two hundred miles south at Sault Ste Marie. To ensure my arrival time, I left home just before six.

Would this be a lengthy trial? How many nights in a hotel before I would see my family? As I hurried into the courtroom, I saw the crown attorney speaking to the defence. The crown seeing me enter the courtroom motioned for me to join them. Then from the crown," Constable, our accused will enter a guilty plea. The proceedings shall be brief. You should be home in time for supper.

Lord Jesus I shall not forget the judge's smile then his whisper to me at the conclusion of presented evidence.

"While I can't enter it into the record, Constable, I know WHO gave you that urge to jump." Lord, this be a reminder to always listen for Your leading?

I Love You Lord – Ron

A Northern Posting

Dear Jesus

We hosted the superintendent's annual visit to our church. The service was well attended. The superintendent delivered the message. After saying farewells, and the last of the congregation having made their way homeward, the three of us headed into the parsonage for a coffee.

After some discussion, he complimented Elaine and me for being so well accepted by both the detachment and the congregation. Then dropped a 'bombshell'. Would we consider a northern posting to a reservation called; Nelson House, Manitoba? Elaine was convinced that White River was to be our springboard to other service for our Lord. Yet this was so soon. Our request to have the night to pray about it was accepted. In the morning it felt right that we should accept the challenge of Nelson House, even though it was not in our list of possibilities, once again as we took this matter to the Lord in prayer, we were reminded of Jeremiah's counsel;

For I know the plans I have for you, declares the Lord, plans for welfare and not for evil, to give you a future and a hope. Jeremiah 29:11

What adventures awaited us in this tiny isolated, perma-frost village?

I love you Lord – Ron

Beyond The Call of Duty

Dear Jesus:

A few days after our arrival. The gentleman Identifying himself as Manitoba Hydro asked if I was familiar with the three 'Cat' diesel generators.? I asked, "who looked after them." Pastor didn't they tell you? You are! We'd better take a walk over to the station." I was surprised at their size. "But I am not a mechanic!" "Pastor, not to worry, these cats run forever on their own. I come in once a month to check to see if everything's running smoothly."

Lord, I don't feel assured. I am not a mechanic; I do not have electrical expertise. How can I be responsible for maintaining power to the village and especially to the nursing station? Lord are You ignoring my plea? I love You Lord, and I really do need to feel your presence in this challenging situation. In later hours I was able to pray; Lord it seems that your guiding hand must have guided me through this turmoil. I made my way to the generator building and, in the desk, I came across a book of which cover someone had scrawled the notation; Cat Maintenance for Dummies. Scanning the pages, I gained enough confidence that I really 'might' be able to take on this responsibility. There were challenging times during the next three years, but I was able to manage the task.

I love You Lord – Ron

You Silly Asses

Dear Jesus:

Over coffee this evening Mrs. Spence mentioned that her mother had just celebrated her 66th birthday hadn't received her Old Age Pension cheque. Well, here we go again I thought. A hearing, where three reputable citizens with established dates of birth, would swear that Mrs. Bonnar was older than they, and since they were over 65 years of age, the applicant met age requirements.

I convened a hearing, and in 'time', a coffee party was called to celebrate the arrival of the first pension cheque. During the celebration, Mrs. Bonnar mentioned; "but my mother still hasn't received her cheque." Now, still a novice in the ways bureaucrats work toward achieving their level of incompetency, I thought this would be relatively simple. The very next week the mail plane brought the department's response; While we recognize that Mrs. Bonnar is presently receiving benefits, and while we recognize that Mrs. Hartie is Mrs. Bonner's <u>natural</u> mother, this is not proof of eligibility ... please convene a hearing" .. I picked up a red felt marker and wrote across the letter; "You silly asses", and without further explanation returned to sender.. By return mail plane, a letter indicated without explanation, "Due to further information received, the applicant is deemed eligible".

I Love You Lord – Ron

Want To Be A Politician

Dear Jesus:

There was a knock on our door. Three strangers, "Pastor Hobden, may we come in?" Reverend, we will get right to the point. As you no doubt know, we are three months away from a provincial election. We have had reports from several sources that you would be the man our party should consider for nomination to this riding."

Silence reigned in the room, finding just the right words, I replied "Gentlemen while your offer is astounding, I am not a politician, nor aspirations to become one." There was some effort to have me rethink my answer, and as it was apparent that they were going to continue on, I felt it was time to end this attempted recruitment.

"Gentlemen, let me frame my answer this way. Were I going to enter the political area, it would be on the side of your political enemies. After a moment of shocked silence, they made" their way to the door and departed. Lord, forgive me if I was too abrupt, but You have called me to preach the Word here.

I Love You Lord – Ron

Suicidal Tendencies

Dear Jesus:

Here in isolation, we were subject to the decisions of department of education officials and especially so with staff appointments. We had grave concerns when notification was received some weeks ago that one of the teachers assigned to us was being released from a psych. hospital. Our principal must keep an eye on her as she may be prone to suicidal tendencies. We questioned, "Why would they send such a 'teacher' into a northern isolated community?" Yet well I knew that we were indeed served by bureaucrats who had attained their maximum level of incompetence.

Her skills became obvious when our son in kindergarten brought home his first report card. It read; 'Brent knows most of the letters of the alphabet and can count to ten.' Elaine nearly lost it! Showing the report to the principal she emphasized; Brent can read children's books; he can count to one hundred in English and he can count to ten in five languages. I want him out of her class. After stressing that she would resign and teach Brent at home, the principal finally consented. Soon it became known in the community that the staff were apprehensive of this 'teacher'. Lord, thank you that the future days are in Your hands.

I love You Lord – Ron

Ron Hobden

Demon Possession

Dear Jesus

This evening, I received a frantic call from the principal. Arriving at the four apartment teacherage, the staff reported; "she's gone berserk, she picked up a large butcher knife, started giggling and waving it around, thrusting it at us". Following the principal into the dwelling, she accosted us waving the knife and laughing. My police training kicked in, pinning her arm, I was able to force the knife from her grasp and force her to the floor. "There's a piece of rope on the fence, "get it". I called. The principal by this time was holding her feet and in a moment one of the teachers appeared with the length of nylon rope. The nursing station had called for an aircraft and we were aware that it would be at least an hour before its arrival. When it arrived, we learned that it wasn't an R.C.M.P. aircraft. For some reason the nurse had called the airbase for a medivac.

While the principal held her to prevent her from biting me. I strapped her into a seat. We started to withdraw. "Oh no, you don't" the pilot decreed, unless the two of you hold her down, we aren't going anywhere." That evening we had a free ride to Thompson where we were met by two police officers. Thank you, Jesus, that it ended without incident or injury. Thank you for your protection.

I love you Lord - Ron

The Election

Dear Jesus:

After church, the village elders as usual gathered in my office to communicate via my short-wave radio with the elders on the isolated reservations. Much of the chatter focused on the coming provincial election. After I had turned down a request to be candidate, the committee approached a pastor in another community. I was asked for my recommend. I suggested they consider they vote in the way he visited their sick in the hospital. My recommendation was passed over the airwaves.

Last evening, we listened as the results indicated the minister had won. Shortly thereafter a celebration was held at the Legion Hall and mention that the "Reverend" had passed out through intoxication. Dear Jesus, should I have accepted the request to accept this position to our provincial government? And Lord He's apparently said that if he didn't win the election, he could always go back to working forty-five minutes a week behind the pulpit. It wasn't until noon today that the reservation votes were counted showing the win was premature. When the "reverend" learned of my suggestion to the elders. I was most definitely not his "favourite person"

I Love You Lord – Ron

Blasphemy

Dear Jesus

    As the float plane taxied for take-off, I thought back to when the superintendent ordered me to instruct a declared atheist, what was expected of him during his son's baptism. For this avowed atheist was to stand before the Lord and the congregation and declare that Jesus was his Lord and Saviour. The Superintendent's words; "It's expected here in the north, I'm ordering you to comply." Words forced themselves from my lips; "You are ordering me to have a man who is not only an unbeliever, but also mocks everything that is holy to testify that Jesus is his Lord and Saviour! That is blasphemy against the Holy Spirit. "I must resign."

    But Lord, I have a wife and family! Lord, we need a roof over us and food on the table. Lord! Then how or why – I do know WHY. At this point in your writing the King reminded you of an article you had read concerning Rose Clapham, a servant in the nineteenth century committed to counselling multitudes of weary laborers to their Saviour. We here in Glory rejoiced as you penned the final thought: O Lord You are my shepherd; you restoreth my soul: You lead me in the paths of righteousness for his name's sake. Though I may walk through the valley I will fear no evil: for thou art with me;" Taking a deep breath. I determined that my Lord was in charge.

I Love You Lord – Ron

Not Red – Maroon

Dear Jesus

Lord, our car finally 'died'. I found a replacement but, it's a red Volkswagen van! Regulations spell out clearly that even though we were responsible for the vehicle's cost, there are guidelines we must follow. Searching the dealerships for a vehicle that would be within our price range, we came across a Volkswagen Van. When I submitted the vehicle to Territorial, my request was turned down due to the van's colour.

It really didn't seem to me to be too 'sporty' for an officer of the Salvation Army yet the Army would not approve the purchase. I contacted division. The Colonel thought for a moment. "Because it's a red Volkswagen van, approval is refused?" "Yes sir". "And you are happy with the price?" "Yes sir" "Well then, by my authority as divisional commander, I hereby declare the colour to be maroon. Maroon is on the approved list. Go ahead and make the purchase". REMEMBER the message of;

Guide me, O thou great Jehovah
Pilgrim through this barren land
I am weak, but thou art mighty
Hold me with thy powerful hand
Bread of heaven, Bread of heaven
Feed me now and evermore.
I Love you Lord, Ron

You Shall Be holy,
For I Am Holy

And I saw a great number standing before the Cross. "Who are those", I asked. "Those are pastors though well intended, made mockery out our Lord's Holy name.

I watched as the pastor approached the pulpit, "How wonderful", I exclaimed. "Just wait". The angel cautioned. The pastor began; On this Christmas Eve, let us welcome Wendy and William as they read our opening scripture;" Two young children attired in what appeared to be Santa Clause pyjamas, waited until the pastor remembering that he had neglected to do so, and after a lengthy apology to the kids and congregation, placed a couple of wooden steps behind the pulpit. Climbing up onto the steps, the children giggled. "Read the scripture:' the pastor whispered. William hesitating called out, "Where is my page"? Wendy glancing about affirmed. I found it. It's under your foot." Recovering his lost page Willy looked for a long moment then exclaimed "I got it". After a long pause, Wendy nudged him and suggested that he read his lines. William looking at his recovered page then seeing his high lined lines began;

There was in the days of Herod, the king of Judea, a certain priest named Zacharias, of the course of Abaya: and his wife was of the daughters of Aaron, and her name was Elis a bath. And they were both right before. God, walking in all the commandments and ordinances of the Lord blameless. Wendy thinking she could do better pushed Willey aside; and took over;

"And they had no child, because Elisabeth was naked, and they both were now well sicken in years. And it came to pass, that he executed the priest's before God's order of his course. Their duty completed the two jumped down from their stools and ran to their families.

What you have seen is typical in countless 'celebrations' of the Saviour's birth. Services to which many who are questioning – looking for a new beginning for their heart and soul, arrive on a quest only to, after viewing a program mocking the Saviour's birth, leave in disgust, perhaps not to enter a church ever again or nor for years. Pastors standing there before the cross shall prior to being escorted through Glory's Gate now feel the pain of those who from this experience, were delayed in accepting the Saviour AND those whose life terminated before the decision and were upon demise escorted for their beginning of a lost eternity.

The Angel then summarized; Throughout the year, to and including special occasions in the church calendar, the primary responsibility of every leader stepping behind a pulpit is to ensure they have prepared for the event, researching diligently the material they plan to present and to do so believing that in their congregation for this service there might be one who is seeking a Saviour. While we are considering the preacher's approach to the pulpit, let us consider the preacher's modern-day apparel. But first the Hebrew ketone: The priestly tunic. Known as the Hebrew ketonet, tunic: was made of pure linen, covering the entire body from the neck to the feet, with sleeves reaching to the wrists. Now consider many present-day pastors, the 'adornment' of those ordained to officiate the Lord's sacrament. It's Sunday morning out steps the pastor ready to proclaim the Holy Word of God, adorned in a short-sleeved shirt, partially covering his numerous tattoos, short pants or trousers with large tears in one or both legs.

The question then is: Has Christendom evolved into a prism of casual approach to Holy Writ OR a flagrant disregard to all things sacred and Holy. This I questioned during a service of "Holy Communion" when a child in arms began screaming when the golden tray containing the consecrated Bread passed by. Whereupon mom called the server back whispering to the child. "Not too many" "And to all this, remember your account of the church 'pastor' who upon viewing a woman 'dancing in the spirit' Picked up a toddler, then holding the child over his head commenced to shake the child violently while yelling; "Do you want to go to Hell?" As the child started to scream the 'pastor' in great jubilation called out; "Praise the Lord, another sinner has repented." Lord, if I am seeing this, as it really is, please close this church before it leads another soul away from Your love and Kingdom.

He Shoots He Scores

Dear Jesus

The telephone rang, "It was Sergeant Roy. "I hear you're a goalie!" "Well Sarg. that was more than a few years ago." "George is down with the flue; we'll have to forfeit. We really need you!" "But I haven't even had skates on for years." "This will be an easy game; We REALLY need you." Pastor, if you are questioning, should a Pastor don the pads might I remind you of former Los Angeles Kings coach Barry Melrose's words:

Standing up for Christ takes a strong man of God. While it has gotten a lot easier for a Christian hockey player to talk about his faith, no teammate wants a player to "turn the other cheek" when a fight breaks out. "They are some of the most fierce competitors in the world." To really know Jesus is to "run the race to win the prize," To really have a personal relationship with Jesus means competing at the top of your game to give God all the glory. But sarge remember, it'll likely be twenty to one, If I'm that lucky." Well Lord, this may prove interesting.

All too soon 6:00 p.m. Saturday was upon me. I made my way to the ice surface. Face-off!

A centre, crossed the blue line, the team's top scorer something in the neighbourhood of sixty goals this season. His shot, By pure luck I blocked it. I could see the kids, ELAINE! my whole family. Elaine's wave didn't seem to be sparked with enthusiasm, more with the dread of impending doom. Most of Dave's teammates were out. Were they my cheering or, jeering section? The refs. whistle, the puck dropped, a breakaway, a goal. We were leading one NOTHING! The faceoff, an intercepted pass, three on two, here it comes! Was I 'puck shy?" The shot, I was in front of it, stopped it, STOPPED it! Grabbed the puck and hung on. A cheer from my "fans". Thank you, Lord, I gasped out. The next shot a goal and the next they were up three one and thankfully the siren ended the first period. The second ended at six to four we were only two goals down. Stepping on the ice for the final twenty minutes, I was strangely 'somewhat calm'. What could they expect, at least it wasn't 20 to 0.?" The period proceeded, A goal, six to five, seven to five, seven to six, a breakaway a shot, saw it coming caught it, and tossed it to a wingman, seconds passed, catching that puck was a shot in the arm to the team, the last five minutes were in the other team's end seven to seven. A score eight –seven FOR US. Then the siren! On the ride home the kids reliving the game play by play. Lord, may I remember this when next time I am called upon to take on mission impossible.

I love You Lord - Ron

Not A Rum & Coke

Dear Jesus

"Ron, Ron', my eyes try to focus then, a nurse, nodded then moved aside. Mom, Dad and Elaine filled my vision. For the next hours, pain! Nurses and loved ones seemed to flash by. Elaine kept our Christian friends briefed and prayers continued from thirteen community churches. It's quiet, doesn't seem to be anyone in the room. Voices, must be in the hallway; Families in the cafeteria for a break?

"He's still with us, don't think he'll make it through the night." WHO won't? ME, I won't make it through the night? AWAKE – Alert - Elaine, the kids, Lord, get me through this". Pain's subsided, "thank you Lord! A Nurse catches my attention. "I'm thirsty". The two nurses at my bedside, surprised look, at each other, at me. "Mr. Hobden, we can't give you a drink, but this will help", moistening my lips. I see her name tag, "Betty, I'm not asking for rum and coke but water would sure be nice." Betty didn't know how to take this. Her patient on death's door is coming up with a joke! "Just a moment, I'll get your doctor." Another movement! Elaine, mom and dad appear. "Ron the doctor says. "you will be off work for at least a month". That pulmonary embolism, you almost didn't make it. You have to be still and allow the Lord to complete your healing. Thank you

I Love You Lord - Ron

Enemy Soldiers

Ron, maybe I should wait until your discharged from hospital to tell you but since everything's okay, I'll chance it. Your neighbour went berserk. He thought he was back in Germany in combat. Thought that your son and his friends were enemy soldiers. He grabbed a shotgun and discharged the weapon.

The boys were just about out of range but David was hit by a pellet. He has a blue mark, but not hurt at all. The police have the man in custody. Now, here's Elaine and your son, the doctor said it was okay for him to come for a moment so you could see that your son's okay."

I recalled a devotional I had read some time ago;

Stating that just because we are under God's care, it doesn't stop the storms from happening all around us. But it does provide strength and protection for every battle we may face. The storms never have full reign, for right in their midst He reminds us: You are held secure by a Mighty God. You may feel some wind, you may hear the loud thunder, and see darkness or rain all around. Know, that doesn't give we who believe, a passport to skip those situations of hurt and pain. But He does cover us, surround us, with His protection and love, we don't face it alone.

I Love You Lord - Ron

The Family of God

Dear Jesus

This Sunday morning, I should have been standing before my congregation, but Lord, thank you for providing us with a relief pastor. As he convened worship, "folks" he said, "after seeing your response and love to Pastors Ron and Elaine and with apologies to our music team, I want to change our opening Hymn to: I'm So Glad I'm A Part of The Family of God. From the congregation, there was a chorus of "Amens!" and "Praise the Lord". The organ and piano summoned the congregation to stand.

> *I'm so glad I'm a part of the family of God*
> *I've been washed in the fountain,*
> *cleansed by His blood!*
> *Joint heirs with Jesus as we travel this sod,*
> *For I'm part of the family, the family of God.*

I now felt that I had some responsibility toward our neighbour that had mistakenly discharged his shotgun toward the children. Sharing my thoughts with Harry, and his nod of approval

I asked that he contact my neighbour's attorney, share my feelings and ask for a trial postponement that I might offer testimony on behalf of the accused. Now we wait and see.

I love You Lord – Ron

The Trial

Dear Jesus:

Six weeks had passed since my discharge from hospital. I was not 100% but I really thanked You for my healing. That afternoon, I sat in Provincial Court listening to the circumstances surrounding the shooting incident of the children. Finally, my neighbour's lawyer stood, "Your Honour, I call as my final witness, Envoy Hobden to the stand. Your honour, Envoy Hobden is the father of the boy that was wounded." His honour frowned, looked puzzled,

"Yes your honour, defence calls as its last witness, Envoy Hobden." Then standing in the witness box, the court clerk handed me the Bible. "Your honour, I request affirmation." Accepting my request, the Judge nodding stated; "Raise your right hand: Do you solemnly affirm that the evidence you are about to give shall be the truth, the whole truth and nothing but the truth?" "I solemnly affirm"

The defence lawyer approached. "Envoy, you are the father of David Hobden?" "I am." The boy who was allegedly wounded and the reason that we are here this afternoon?' "I am." And you wish to testify on behalf of

Ron Hobden

the accused?" "I do." Shaking his head, the judge said, "proceed". "Your honour, I have known the accused for nearly two years. We have occasionally chatted over the fence. I have come to know that he served with distinction in combat. Your honour, I truly believe that in his mind he was back on active duty at the front. That he was fighting for the freedom of his country, freedom for those of us in this court. Your honour, this could have been a tragedy, I could have lost my son, but as I ask myself, did he shoot at those children? I must say NO! He shot at what he determined was enemy soldiers attempting to take our freedom. I would hope that if the court determines guilt that it will consider hospitalization rather than the Correctional Centre." With no objection from the crown. The Judge nodded, thought for just a moment and pronounced, rather than a term of incarceration in the provincial jail an indeterminant sentence to a psychiatric facility. This being all the matters of the day, this court is closed. As the judge left the room the court clerk asked if I might wait a moment. After arranging her papers, she asked: "Envoy I am not a church girl, but after hearing your testimony, I'd like to attend this Sunday. What time is your service? And pastor, don't be surprised if I am accompanied by his Honour.

As my mind was attempting to sort out the happenings of the day, my memory went back to the days I was a police officer. I had never made a request to offer testimony for the accused. And also never received a request from a court clerk for our worship time. Lord may your healing hand touch that troubled mind. As usual I had closed with;

I love You Lord – Ron

Animal Sacrifice
in Church

Appearing Mother Teresa "Ron, you have recorded another experience of 'tainted worship' in your diary." I recalled only too well the sadness as I penned what I perceived as; Blasphemy of the Holy Spirit. The incidental evil thought or resentment towards God does not count as blasphemy. Although it is a sin, but the fact that it is not persevering and purposeful, deems it to be a forgivable sin. Now to the blasphemy! I recall the vice chair of our church board openly urging that we commence the practice of animal sacrifice.

I opened my Bible to Matthew: 12:31. Jesus said, *"Truly I tell you, people can be forgiven all their sins and every slander they utter"* but then He gives one exception: *"Whoever blasphemes against the Holy Spirit will never be forgiven; they are guilty of an eternal sin"* HOWEVER, let us leave this matter in the hands of the King for He alone knows one's heart and the final judgement of the soul.

My level of astonishment beyond my comprehension as the church chairman and council unanimously agreed that while it wouldn't be appropriate to begin animal sacrifices in the sanctuary they saw no reason to suspend their vice chairman's membership in the church nor from his role on council. This being their decision

And a definite happening, Elaine and I had no alternative but to tender our resignations.

From The Underground to The Salvation Army

Dear Jesus:

Six months have passed since our leaving Nelson House. First, You led me to seek a job in of all places (for me) a mine! Guiding my hands and thoughts, you prepared me for a promotion which led me to be responsible for a squad of miners. You guided me to introduce one of my crew to You. Surely all Glory offered praise as he committed his life to You, Lord. I recall our first Sunday in Thompson, we headed for church.

Upon arrival, a sign, "Closed for the Summer."

Elaine suggested, "well, we have met the Salvation Army officers, why not go there?" Lord were those words that came from Elaine's lips, hers OR were they Yours? Arriving at the Salvation Army Hall we were well received. As the service progressed, our comfort increased.

On the second Sunday, I was asked if I would preach the following Sunday. That afternoon following service, we were invited to the Corp Officer's home for lunch.

After the meal Bruce with a large smile yet with serious word, had a most startling question:

Ron – Elaine, I have been in constant touch with our headquarters about the two of you, your faith to our Lord and your proclamation of The Word.

I Have been asked by our Divisional Commander to ask if you would be interested in accepting an appointment as Corps Officers to Kenora Ont?"

Enrolment Into
The Army

Dear Jesus

Lord In two weeks, we shall stand behind Your pulpit again – Your pulpit! Lord. I don't understand? Do You have a sense of humour? Whatever lies before us, I ask You to take control. Then I had a thought. We have been appointed as Corps Officers yet have never joined the Salvation Army. We rushed over to the officer's quarters. "Bruce, we are appointed to Kenora" "Yes, isn't that wonderful, Praise the Lord." "Shouldn't we be at least members of the Army?" Bruce gasped and picked up the telephone. In a moment he relayed my question to the divisional commander. Bruce listened for a moment then "I'm to give you a crash course, enrol you as Salvationists. So began the next five years of our ministry.

Grandma Gamble broke my Holy Silence. "Ron", she mentioned "These songs of praise 'twigged my conscience to another choir, this time a makeshift choir composed of family. Your family offering songs of praise. When the Lord stretched out His hand and rescued you from drowning at Little Detroit. Consider your new appointment. This is beyond even a fantasy. From an underground nickel miner to an Officer in the Salvation Army. This is impossible! However, you now know that nothing is impossible when the King of Kings determines that it shall be so. How proud were your parents;

At this new appointment I was blessed with a large office and, it was a necessity, for much of our work involved 'social services' as homeless folks passing through stopped in for meal vouchers. One afternoon I counted twenty awaiting a meal ticket. As well as the strangers we had locals asking for assistance. I recall one afternoon Isaac, a twenty-year-old who was said to have an allergy to any type of work, arrived. Isaac was no stranger, at least once a week often more he'd drop in and demand a meal ticket. On this occasion I was involved in preparation for a Bible study. My Bible was open on my desk to second Thessalonians, chapter three. Later I would reminisce that this whole event had to have been planned by our Lord. Seeing my open Bible on my desk. Isaac demanded; "Preacher, I want you to do what that book says. Give me a meal ticket." "Isaac, do you want me to do what this book says?" With a note of impatience, he gave a brief nod. "Isaac do you really want me to do what this book says?" to which his response bordered upon hostility. Turning my Bible around, with affirmation I replied, "Today, I shall do exactly what this book tells me to do. Listen to verse ten:

> For even when we were with you, we gave you this rule: "The one who is unwilling to work shall not eat."

"Isaac, I shall do as you asked. There shall be no voucher for you today.

I Love You Lord – Ron

Elaine's Prayer

Dear Jesus

Ron has severe chest pains and been diagnosed with a pulmonary embolism. He continued over the next days to have a series of blood clots move through and the prognosis was grim. I, of course prayed fervently. BUT… my prayers consisted of, "Lord save him. Lord, why me? Lord, I need my husband. I have four boys who need their father. Notice the emphasis? I, prayed and I fretted. I lost twenty pounds in two weeks! Then the wife of one of the pastors came to visit. She brought a can of cookies for the children, (we had 7 between 1 year and 14). On the can she had printed the following words: Isaiah 43:1-3.

When you go through deep waters and great trouble, I will be with you. When you go through rivers of difficulty, you will not drown! When you walk through the fire of oppression, you will not be burned up– the flames will not consume you. For I am the Lord your God, your Savior, the Holy One of Israel.

I spent the following two hours on my knees. It was when I came to the decision that I COULD continue, that I knew God was able, that I was willing to say, "Lord, whatever happens, I WILL serve you. If you take Ron, I will praise You; If you spare him, I will thank you." Then I received the peace which only You, my Lord, can give.

I love You Lord   Elaine

Be Healed

Dear Jesus

Lord, I understand that physical healing is your most common miracle. Were those biblical events specific to that place and time? Undoubtedly, Lord they were part of your ministry of signs and wonders, which points each of us to You as Messiah with authority to restore creation. You are unchanging, but is Your promise that miracles still happen today? And to me personally? Lord, in wonder I heard the doctor's words.

Dr. Brenda's examination was telling. "Ron, I can't say that you are healed. Your condition can't be written off for at least five years of freedom from your diagnosed condition. But I can say that this is nothing short of miraculous." Now Lord I wondered. What lies ahead, I have no idea, but I do know that under your control, the impossible is always possible,

Ibarashi interjected into my thoughts; "Your greatest gift is the woman the Lord provided to be your helpmate. As you, she deeply loves her Lord. She is a woman committed to prayer. Now recall the moment when after hours on her knees before her Lord, Elaine glanced at your diary then penned her prayer to her Lord: All there is for one to say is that The Lord heard your beloved's prayer and ordered a miracle

I love You Lord – Ron

Evan

My Father's thoughts broke into the holy silence of my home for all eternity. I see that the word in your diary indicate that thus far your ministry has led a number of seekers, as well as those in opposition to the Saviour to Him. At the King's direction there was a hush, as Evan's drama, as recorded within your diary, unfolded.

Dear Jesus

I heard the office door opening it was a very troubled Evan. Captain, could you pray for me. I led him into our church and he fell down in front of the altar and he prayed for forgiveness. We remained on our knees for almost two hours. I can still see the tears were running down his cheeks as he left my office.

Sunday morning Evan stood. He told everyone about the meeting he had with me and his prayer at the altar asking God to forgive him. He looked so happy, he had gone to his boss and he asked his boss to forgive him. He then told us he telephoned the former pastor and asked for his forgiveness then they had prayer on the telephone. Then

Evan said that he had hurt many people here in the church, could they forgive him? There was silence

Someone began to sing; 'They'll Know We are Christians by Our Love.' I nodded to the organist, she began to play, we began to sing.

There was such a feeling of forgiveness and love. I didn't preach a sermon that morning. I asked the congregation to just gather in small groups and talk to each other. To share Jesus' love. They talked, they prayed, they cried they laughed. Many asked others to forgive them for hurt feelings and for bitterness' that had separated people in some instances for years. The sin of bitterness gone. God's forgiveness not only filled Evan's heart that morning, but so many others made peace as well. There was peace in the church that Sunday morning.

My benediction included the richness of the Apostle Luke's words; "I tell you that in the same way there will be more rejoicing in heaven over one sinner who repents than over ninety-nine righteous persons who do not need to repent." Luke 15:7 to which the Angelic Choir responded; Halleluiah, he who was lost has been found. To which the King responded: To he\she taking my Word to the lost, the struggling, it is written in the pages of My Holy Writ. Let the Sower of the seed consider:

> The parables of The Lost Sheep,
> The Lost Coin, and
> The Lost Son

The three parables of the lost being found illustrate My kindness and My mercy. When those who are lost are found, there is much rejoicing in all My household.

I Love You Lord – Ron

Careless Words

Dear Jesus:

Was this morning's devotional, focusing upon James: a note of caution to this pastor?

All kinds of animals, birds, reptiles and sea creatures are being tamed and have been tamed by mankind, but no human being can tame the tongue. James 3:7-8a

Then Lord, a thought! Perhaps I am to consider James words as advice for the simple everyday transactions in my life? Upon which, I recalled a recent incident at one of the city's car dealerships. One of our doctors, on his day off was doing some construction in his back yard.

Dressed in jeans and a tee shirt, he drove over to the Ford dealership. As 'fate' would have it, the doctor was approached by a new salesperson eager to make a sale but not so eager to waste his time on a non-productive car-gazer. The doctor approached the novice salesman with; "Good afternoon, I'm doctor Peter Pan and I want to place an order for a Ford Thunderbird and a Lincoln." The salesman quipped, "I'm Mickey mouse and I'd like a Porch and a Mac truck." The doctor walked out of the dealership, drove to the

G.M. dealership and ordered a Cadillac for his wife and a corvette for himself. Lord, as Your pastor, may I with your guidance be always in control of my tongue.

I Love You Lord Ron.

Ron Hobden

The Grizzly

As I gazed at the tree of life, Dennis appeared. "I was recalling your diary entry about the night of the grizzly.

Dear Jesus – You wrote:

Here in Golden a huge grizzly bear has been making life miserable for us. Whenever I yell at him, he challenges me. I called the R.C.M.P. and they said; "shoot him".

This evening we had a B.B.Q. for our church board. Seeing a movement out of the brush, I noted that our four-footed friend obviously smelling the cooking meat decided he'd join the activity. As the balcony was just a couple of steps above ground level, it seemed prudent for us to move indoors.

A moment passed, then, the griz. hit our kitchen door. Opening a closet, I handed my rifle to Bill, our board chairman and grabbed my 12-gauge shotgun and a couple of slugs. This was surely the first time I was about to interrupt a church board meeting with gun-fire. The grizzly hit the door again. I motioned to the door handle, Bill nodded and aimed the rifle, As I swung open the door, Bill's shot was immediately followed by my own. No one wanting the carcass; the following morning, I would haul it off to the dump. Dear Lord I guess this ends my day. And thank you that no one was injured.

I Love You Lord – Ron

Betrayed Trust

Dear Jesus:

"Lord, how must we deal with this betrayal? This evening at our first church board meeting, the board was surprised to hear that Elaine was planning to serve as pastor. They had met with the superintendent and clearly voiced their disapproval to a female behind their pulpit. He had advised that he'd deal with it, that it wouldn't be a problem. Yet there wasn't even a hint in all our communication, written or verbal of the matter. I explained our stand on this issue, together with ample proof from God's Word.

Turning to the most adamant member, I quoted: "For God so loved the world that he gave his one and only Son, that whoever believes in him shall not perish but have eternal life." John 3:16 and asked if he was in agreement with this text. "Pastor, he muttered, "This church knows, that that is the only way to salvation." "Is this for everyone," I countered. Everyone spoke out or confirmed by nodding. Then I cautioned, "but this surely applies only to we men. Would you please stand and read 1Timothy 2:15. Somehow, he'd missed recalling this text, standing, he flipped open his Bible and began; "But women will be saved through childbearing - if they continue in faith, love and holiness with propriety." "So, as it is the board's contention that scripture is to be accepted without question and literally, do you invoke John 3:16 and discount Timothy 2:15? May I remind you that as Elaine an ordained pastor in the church has given birth to six children 1 and has also embraced John 3:16 thus she has met the requirements of God's Word." I would also suggest a secret ballot, allowing each of you to respond according to your heart. There was complete silence as we left the room. Twenty minutes later our presence was requested. I noticed that there were two empty chairs. The chairman's comments echoed a sigh of relief.

The ballots were counted, it was six to two in favour of a request that we remain as pastors. There had been a division in the board for years as to female preachers. The majority of the congregation were hesitant to stand against the two families in the church. While they would miss the two dissenting families, some believed that these 'archaic' attitudes were the cause of their dwindling congregation. The chairperson looked toward us, "Pastors would one of you close this meeting with prayer. Elaine gave me a nod, Pausing for a moment I voiced the words of a recent prayer; "Teach us thy way, O Lord, of providence, grace, and duty; Lead us on a straight path. Guide us on the path of truth that helps us understand and find knowledge; that shows us the way of holiness, the path of righteousness, in which Christ, the shepherd of his people, leads us. Lord, we come to you for healing.

I love You Lord – Ron

Attendance Statistics

Dear Jesus:

We met with the council chairman. He was amazed at the attendance report that I'd received from the Bishop. "Pastor", he exclaimed; "our average Sunday attendance struggles to be in the high forties, not the seventies your report shows. Thirty-five for evening service! We haven't had an evening service for at least a few years. Sunday School in the forties. There isn't a Sunday School class. Usually, the pastor calls the four or five children to the front for a story after the announcements. And pastor; all this was discussed with the bishop during his last visit as we considered calling you to come as our pastor". Lord, I must admit that this shocking news isn't new to me. O Lord how many church leadership personnel will upon judgement day hear your tragic words; "Depart from Me, I never knew you."

Heavenly Father may each of Your servants from recently ordained to cardinal, from pastor to bishop understand the importance of putting Your interests first, self-interests last! May they understand their responsibility to maintain a life of holiness together with blessings beyond measure that Your Word may flourish within Your servants, congregations, and community.

I Love You Lord – Ron

Stressed Leadership

Dear Jesus:

The folk now warmly accept Elaine as their pastor, we now feel comfortable in Golden. We might continue on here until retirement, perhaps several years away. We purchased an acreage a few miles out of the community. We marvelled and visitors were awed by the spectacular view of the majestic snow-capped mountains. O Lord, I have received devastating news this week. One of our leaders has been discovered as having inappropriate conduct with a teen. It is under investigation and the police have advised that I must keep the information that has come to me confidential. It cannot be made known prior to a trial. When I informed our bishop, I was instructed that until the matter is resolved before the court, the accused must be barred from all leadership within the church's ministry. Following the bishop's instructions, I called a congregational meeting whereupon, I gave each board member a copy of the bishop's fax, waited for a few moments for them to absorb the content then read the bishop's fax to the congregation. Several demanded answers of which I was not at liberty to divulge, whereupon a third of the gathering walked out. Lord, only you know how this is going to end. Lord we need, I need your guidance and assurance. Lord help us, help your church.

I love You Lord – Ron

Captain, Your
House is Burning

Dear Jesus

A beautiful spring day greeted us as we left the house and headed out to campaign for Red Shield. A half hour passed, then the C.B. radio. "Captain your house is burning" Grabbing the mike I responded; "whose house?" "Captain it's your house." We made a quick U-turn. The fire men were already on hand. After the flames were extinguished only a burned-out shell remained. What happened here? Well, Charlie heard an explosion and swears that the house jumped a foot or two off its foundation.

I stood in shock; the furnace had evidently exploded. After the shock started to wear off, we realized that we had no clothes, very minimal funds and no roof over our heads. I called our insurance agent. "Ron," he said, "you owe me ninety dollars. I tried to convince you to increase your coverage. Well, when you left my office, I was concerned about your protection. I increased your coverage to $8000.00, not much but at least an improvement. I'll be there as soon as I can. Don`t worry, I`ll book you in at the hotel I can give you an advance to get you started."

My next call was to our divisional officer. "Brigadier, I`m going to ask the Fire Chief to notify the Fire Marshal that I`d like to have an investigation. Our children could have been killed. We need to know what happened". "No", he replied, "they might find that the Army was responsible. No you are not to do that." Hanging up the phone, I decided that I just had to defy him.

The Fire Chief called. The investigation into cause of the fire now completed: Apparently there was a mix-up at the terminal. The fuel truck was equipped with three tanks; the first for aviation fuel, the second for gasoline the third oil for home furnaces. There was a mix-up between the first and third tanks. Our tank was filled with aviation fuel. I telephoned our divisional officer, "Sir, the band has offered us temporary use of an empty reservation house. The toilet has to be replaced and I'm requesting authorization to spend $99.00 for a toilet for our quarters. First he acknowledged what he thought was good news about the fuel mix-up and there was no way the Army would be at fault. Then to show his anger toward me for disobeying his instruction, he refused permission; "There's a Shell Station just across the street, you and your family use their toilet." Hanging up the telephone in shock, I dialled the number for his superior. When the Colonel answered, I briefed him of the situation. I was assured that the matter would be taken care off. "But sir", I responded, "I no longer have any faith nor respect for my divisional officer, if we cannot be transferred out of his division, I must tender my resignation. It is time for us to leave!" The next day we received orders to move to North Battleford. Saskatchewan.

Thank you, I Love you Lord – Ron

Farewell

Dear Jesus:

It is with a heavy heart that I back out of the driveway and we head east to a new appointment. As I considered the past year, I wondered how long we might to able to continue serving in this work that we loved so dearly and in spite of all its challenges, were still committed so intensely. Thank you, Lord, for the many joys we have experienced. For the privilege of bringing the lost into your family. Thank you for providing us with the strength to deal with the hand of opposition that so often came upon us. Lord, we have knowledge of despicable acts, yet are unable to make things right.

Surely the events and circumstances that confronted us over the past months, light fixtures that were stolen from an abandoned church and installed in the church being renovated, financial records that we were forbidden to examine; Our buying a car upon the assurance from our supervisor that it was in perfect working order, then later advised that it had been written off after an accident; a pastor's son who for insurance had repeatedly struck his car with a hammer to simulate hail damage; our family with six children, for over a month having to use the sink and washroom facilities in a service station down the street. Lord, the list seemed almost endless, yet we have felt Your hand upon us.

I Love You Lord - Ron

I Believe, Help My Unbelief

Dear Jesus

O Lord, I believe, help my unbelief. Dear Jesus, where are You leading us? First, I, with great excitement accepted the challenge of a call to overseas missions as a Christian hospital in Papa New Guinea was in need of a missionary director. The 'challenge' was that to fulfil that role, I needed to be either a medical doctor or at least an R.N. Well, the time required to become a medical doctor was unrealistic. However, with assurance that my placement would be waiting and the need vital, I with great anxiety, entered nursing college. The first year passed by and with great anticipation the first two months of the final year progressed. Then a national news broadcast: Terrorists in Papa New Guinea had stormed a hospital. It was believed that thirty of the hospital staff were executed. A call to the international office confirmed the tragedy. The following week came news of the mission's permanent closure. With great sadness, I withdrew from my studies, and accepted a position with the department of Justice in La Ronge Saskatchewan.

Lord is my life to have meaning? Lord has the joy of opportunity for me to stand behind a pulpit and preach Your Word gone from my life? Have I somehow failed and am being punished? If You are still with me, Lord let me feel your hand upon me. I do Love You Lord – Ron

Seemingly Ridiculous

A year has passed; crippling arthritis demanded sick leave. As the days and weeks ensued, our pastor urged that I was indeed called into the ministry of the Word and Sacrament, I should consider seminary. This seemed ridiculous! With at times, a pain so severe that I didn't crawl out of bed until near noon, How could I even consider sitting in a classroom?

Lord what alternative do I have, but we leave this in Your hands? Lord, I felt for the first time in a while Your presence. The pastor's message first, then a very special chorus that seemed wholly directed toward me. The words of our closing chorus:

> I know who holds the future,
> And I know he holds my hand;
> So as I face tomorrow
> with its problems large and small,
> I'll trust the God of miracles,
> Give to Him my all.

As fall classes loomed, the pastor's needling continued. Finally, I determined I would have an interview just to prove the pastor wrong. I arrived at Dr. Nostbakken's office and was warmly welcomed. I explained; "There are times when I'm unable to sit in a chair". "Then stand at the back of the classroom where we will place a stool for added support." What about the days when my pain is so severe that I don't get out of bed until noon?" "Then by all means stay in bed.

When you feel up to class, a time can be arranged by the instructor to bring you up to speed." And on and on it went. That Sunday morning's service seemed to be directed toward me. And, Lord, the final 'straw' was the chorus of a closing hymn resounded in my thoughts: I'll go where You want me to go, dear Lord.

That Monday morning, I enrolled for the fall session. The year passed, a year of profound praise to my Lord as I was now convinced that this was surely His leading and in the near future the Free Methodist Church. Then Aldersgate College in Moosejaw, Saskatchewan. The following year Elaine, accepting God's calling enrolled alongside me.

I Love You Lord – Ron

Rape Fantasies

Dear Jesus:

It was with a great deal of uncertainty that I enrolled in Aldersgate College to complete the requirements for a B.Th. It would desperately stretch our resources. The only word that came to light was 'bankruptcy', yet both Elaine and I felt strongly that this was God's calling. My second class this morning was English Literature. As the lesson progressed, professor Lori handed out our semester assignment. I looked at the outline and gasped. I glanced at a couple of classmates and could see that we were on "the same page". I raised my hand, was acknowledged, stood and as respectfully as I could manage, I stated. "This assignment is an evaluation of Margret Attwood's Rape Fantasies?" "It is."" Professor, I cannot comply." "Mr. Hobden, it is a course requirement. I calmly as I could manage, replied. It is my understanding that this is a college with a mandate to teach the Word of our Lord not the filth that is expected in this assignment. I must refuse. I would challenge you to give me a failing grade."

Our professor stood in shocked silence for a moment then walked out of the classroom. Three classmates were standing beside me as the principal walked in. Briefly advising the assignment "Rape Fantasies" would be removed from studies."

I Love You Lord – Ron

It's Time For Us To Withdraw

Dear Jesus:

Our account with the college is in arrears. The only thing we can think of, is that it's time to increase our giving." We wrote our Sunday offering. Then I paused, it was, time to inform the college that we must withdraw. With a heavy heart I made my way to the college business office. "Don, have you a moment"

Don listened as I explained our financial situation. "Even if all goes well, we will be a thousand dollars short of making it through to graduation." Don interrupted; "Ron, the board surmised your situation and I was about to call you in to assure you not to worry, we are not concerned about your account. Let's just leave this in His hands".

As Elaine was preparing lunch the telephone rang, A stranger, spoke "I have a cheque for $ 1000 for you, would you like to come and pick it up"? We picked it up! What we needed to understand is that when we trust God, there is no need to fear what life may throw at us. After lunch as Elaine was cleaning up I overheard her softly singing a familiar tune. Listening closely;

This little light of mine, I'm gonna let it shine.

Let it shine, let it shine, let it shine. Let it shine till Jesus comes, I'm going to let it shine Lord, thank you –

I love you Lord – Ron

God Told Me You Needed This

Dear Jesus:

So often we wonder where our next dollar is coming from. I know Lord that when we felt all was lost and resigned ourselves that we must pull out of studies You intervened by providing those dollars for our spring tuition.

Now we have been careful with our budget. Yet in spite of our carefulness, I woke up this morning with dread as I considered that we wouldn't have enough gas in our tank to make it to church. But suddenly I felt calm, I seemed to have assurance that it was okay, that we should head out the hundred and fifty miles to File Hills. I know it didn't make sense, but while we were really apprehensive, we headed east. For some reason, I felt that I shouldn't mention our financial plight to the congregation this morning. After I pronounced the benediction. My feeling of uneasiness, actually Lord, fright, returned. That morning we had an American couple on their way to Toronto join us for worship. Now Lord, this was way off the route for Toronto but they said they had driven the usual way and this time thought they'd take a scenic route. As I shook the gentleman's hand he passed me a note. "God told me you needed this he whispered. Folded in the note a twenty-dollar bill. Enough to make it home and a couple of dollars to spare.

I Love You Lord – Ron

The Saint James Bible

Dear Jesus:

On my first Sunday at Roblin, Manitoba, I was with anxiety. I had promised to follow the bishop's direction. Opening my bible. "Hear the Word of the Lord. This morning from the New International Version". One of the old guard stood, "We will have none of that in this church. We hear only the word of God from the authorized St. James Bible" "Sir I responded please sit down." His response; "Blasphemy, We shall have none of that in this church." To which I responded; "Sir, on the authority of the Bishop, you will sit down or you will be removed from this church." There were a few gasps from the congregation and a few smiles as the elder slumped to his seat.

"My friends in Christ; I received direction from our bishop. What I am about to relate to you is new to me. I trust our bishop explicitly and it is my fervent hope that you do also; I am to inform you that for the future proclamation of the gospel of our Saviour, a few changes must be made. While we recognize The King James Bible; we also have several other translations of God's Holy Word. While each member should rely upon their preference, including the King James for their private study. The bishop suggests thought be given to the N.I.V in corporate worship. An arctic blast of cold air was felt.

I Love You Lord – Ron

Carnal Knowledge

Dear Jesus:

The following Sunday I passed on the bishops further advice. He has received several comments that the cupboards in the church kitchen are locked, restricting access to a chosen few. He requests that the locks be immediately removed for accessibility to all involved in kitchen service to the congregation. Further, I am advised that we shall have further directions concerning other matters from our bishop for consideration, in the weeks to come. Following the benediction, the congregation made their way from the church in silence.

Lord, we are going to really need Your guidance over these next few days and weeks.

Our church is based upon the truth of the Holy Word and for Your glory. But, how often do we pray for the peace and purity of the congregation? How often do we pray for the peace and purity of we who are your local body? Perhaps Lord if we should all pray more often for the unity grounded in gospel essentials.

Sadly, we have lost a couple of families of seniors from the bishop's edict on modern translations of scripture. Yet, sources within the community indicate a positive reversal of attitude toward some searching a church home.

This evening, the board discussed and voted on the bishop's recommendation to close the segregated beaches in favour of the city pool.

"It's long overdue" was the response. "Pastor were you aware that during summer camp for swimming the boys and girls swam from separate beaches AND at different times." "The purpose? Why, are the elementary kiddies segregated? "Pastor," his hand raised in helpless gesture, "our children have been restricted to gender to prevent carnal knowledge". In utter disbelief I questioned; "So children as young as four years of age are kept segregated to prevent an accelerated awareness of carnal knowledge"? In reply to my question, a helpless nod.

Following the vote, I was asked if I'd be willing to drive the bus that we might transport BOTH boys and girls together to the city swimming pool. A responsibility I took on without hesitation. Lord, may this be the moment when the community sees our church coming out of the 'dark ages.' Our church has been long shunned even by the Christian community. Of note is the fact that, in spite of being yelled at, that they were on their way to Hell, two teen age granddaughters of the 'old guard' have been wearing miniskirts to church in rebellion. Lord, I trust that the board and congregation are ready to open their hearts and minds to Your leading.

I love You Lord – Ron

A Fifty Dollar Bill

Dear Jesus:

Lord, I need Your guidance as the investigation continues. Cherelle's mother had given her a fifty-dollar bill which she had placed on the car seat beside her. Opening the window, a draft blew the bill down onto the floor. Reaching down to retrieve the money she took her eyes of the narrow gravel sideroad for a second, yet that second was enough.

I saw her car approaching well across the centre of the road and I pulled over to the edge of the highway, sounded my horn, managed to stop just as the two vehicles collided. Thank you, Lord that while Cherelle's injuries required her be transported to the hospital they were not life threatening. Our car was written off by our insurance.

After the ambulance had left the scene, I urged the police officer to be as lenient as he could. That Cherelle was not reckless, he nodded but affirmed that he must write a charge of careless driving. Later in the day after visiting her parents and assuring them that neither Elaine nor I were injured, and how concerned we were that Cherelle's broken arm would quickly heal, that if the matter ever went to court, we'd be very willing to serve as witnesses of Cherelle's character. Thank you –

I love You Lord - Ron

Is Japan Calling?

Dear Jesus:

Two years have passed since we first arrived in Roblin. While progress into the modern era has been slow, the congregation has been blessed with some measure of welcome by the Christian community.

Acceptance and support for using the city swimming pool now established and welcomed. A few young families noticing the welcome mat open, have ventured to join us for Sunday worship. Except for funerals, rarely do we see the 'old guard' in attendance. They remain within our prayer lists.

During the last couple of weeks, I have received two letters in the mail, the first from the Bishop supporting our stand, stating that he sees both spiritual and numerical growth in the congregation, the second a refusal for a transfer to the Ontario congregation we had requested.. Lord, we ask, what is your leading? We are ready to commit as in the words of our most recent guiding song writer, Mary Brown.

We will go where You want us to go, dear Lord, o'er mountain, or plain, or sea; we'll be what You want us to be. But if, by a still, small voice he calls to paths that we do not know, I'll answer, dear Lord, with my hand in thine: I'll go where you want me to go. Do we remain here or overseas? We await Your leading

I love you Lord – Ron

His Plans for Our Future

As the notes of praise ebbed from the cherubim choir, Ibarashi, my spiritual guide, appeared at my side. "I see that you were recalling excerpts from your diary. Consider for a moment, your healing." Consider how the Saviour's plan for your future high lights the words of the prophet Jeremiah:" Consider how He put His plan for your future into action. Consider now my counsel; Let your diary be opened!

"For I know the plans I have for you, declares the Lord, plans to prosper you and not to harm you, to give you a future and a hope." NOW open your diary:"

Dear Jesus

Lord, I couldn't understand! First my hands lost their grip. Then my legs no longer carried my weight. We Traded our motorcycle for a video camera. Gave up skydiving and became a couch potato. After a while the doctor found a delicate balance between fogging my brain too heavily with drugs and keeping me lucid. It was then that I found myself in seminary. I was aware You were calling me to return to the pastorate, but I procrastinated and time went by. In seminary my caring and loving wife lifted me before You on those days when the pain made it impossible. You taught me how to cope. I was provided with a computer.

I Love You Lord – Ron

Ron Hobden

So you will know

Dear Jesus:

My first year at Roblin completed, we went to our church camp. I lay awake in bed, unable to sleep because of the pain. I got up and went down to the beach and prayed; "Lord if I must continue to experience this pain, I will do what You want me to do. The minutes passed then, suddenly, I felt very warm. Everything seemed to be so very quiet. It was wonder beyond human comprehension. A thought, a whisper touched my brain..' "So you will know!"

The call of the gulls overhead broke the silence. I felt a breeze coming off the lake. Picking up my canes, I started back toward our cabin. In shock, I was aware that there was no pain. Lord, I don't understand, but You took away the pain. Lord, that was two years ago. Have You healed me permanently? Have You freed me from my dark valley that I might better serve You. However, that must not be my concern. One thing I do know, my future is in Your Hands and with that I am content.

Lord, I understand that physical healing is your most common miracle. Were those biblical events specific to that place and time? Undoubtedly, yes! Lord they were part of your ministry of signs and wonders, which points each of us to You as Messiah with authority to restore

Creation. I Love You Lord – Ron

Lifted From My Burden

Dear Jesus

I understand that physical healings are your most common miracles. They have been and are part of your ministry of signs and wonders, pointing each of us to You as Messiah.

Dr. Brenda's examination was telling. "Ron, I can't say that you are healed. Your condition can't be written off for at least five years of freedom from your diagnosed condition. But I can say that this is nothing short of miraculous."

"Lord what lies ahead? I have no idea! But I do know that under your control, the impossible is always possible, Lord your healing would be prominent in our accepting this calling this new adventure for the Kingdom.

Appearing at my side, Elaine's dad nodded,

I see that you have now recalled another healing touch of the master. Another 'touch' that signalled you were to be about your assigned business. We awaited your future exploits from the master. We rejoiced as you introduce each soul to the Master. Now my son, open your diary to your words of Japan Calling. As my diary appeared before me with page opened I gazed at the entry I had made many decades before yet a moment ago here in Glory

I Love You Lord – Ron

Wanted in Japan

Dear Jesus:

We feel you are calling us to prepare for a new field of service. Then this evening after service as Elaine was preparing supper, the telephone rang. I listened in disbelief, "Just a moment" I replied to the stranger's voice. "Honey, it's the church's director of foreign missions, They want us in Japan" "Japan, no way!" "But sir!" "Listen pastor, this is not of my doing, somehow, the folks in Nishinomiya have heard about you. For months they have been lifting their need for a pastor to the Lord. One of our English instructors was a fellow classmate at Aldersgate with you. She explained to the church about your opposition to a class assignment; 'Rape Fantasies. Your willingness to give up everything for the Lord, so convinced them that God has chosen you and Elaine, that they have placed a very large deposit on a rental house FOR YOU."

SOMEHOW we had a sudden feeling that the Lord's Hand was in this "Sir can we have a week to think and pray about this. Hanging up the phone I turned to Elaine, "YES, We pray but for this we need outside support." We thought, then I suggested, "Seven is a good number, let's call seven folks that we know. They will in all sincerity take this to our Lord." Elaine picked up a pen, we made a list; our parents, former students from Aldersgate, and a couple from the church. To each we explained our dilemma. "Does our Lord really want us to go to Japan?

Now, we don't ask that you would pray for writing in the sky or a phone call from the Lord." We asked that they take this to our Lord and then we'd call again early Sunday evening and ask if they had a feeling of peace about it?"

The week passed. I began calling. The first five confirmed they were at peace with our going. I called Elaine's mom who I knew would be ecstatic. "How can I support you?" Then, with deep concern I dialled my parents' number. I knew that my father would respond, "Ron, are you out of your mind. JAPAN, you might be away for years. What if something happened to one OR both of you? You don't know any of those strangers." The phone was ringing, Dad answered, "Mother and I have taken this to our Lord each day. We are concerned that you had really better think carefully about this before you turn it down!" Three months later, strangers, picked us up at the Osaka airport. Again, we respond to: I'll go where You want me to go, dear Lord, O'er mountain or plain or sea; I'll be what You want me to be Lord! We have no idea, how or even why???

We love you Lord – Ron

The Adventure Begins

A movement – It's Charles Wesley. "Ron I enjoy your diary. May we open it's pages to your initial time in the land of the Rising Sun. It wasn't long until you began to refer to the land As "The Rising SON" "Here it is."

Dear Jesus

The three-hour flight to Vancouver followed by a two hour wait, then an eight-hour flight to the Land of the Rising 'Son'. After passing through immigration, we soon spotted a sign, "HOBDENS". It was our welcoming committee. Two friendly strangers, but strangers that would in just days become friends.

After a ninety-minute drive we pulled up at a small cottage, and following our guides, who unlocked the door and motioned for me to lead the way into our 'new home'. On the kitchen table a card of greeting. On the stove, a coffee perk, cups, sugar, milk and coffee. We thanked them for their kindness and Elaine's offer to have a coffee was accepted. Twenty minutes later they said farewell, and, this was our introduction to Japan. Lord, we prayed, if You really mean for us to even be here; we shall rely on Your help to keep us from committing blunders which will be a detraction and detrimental to our ministry. Lord, we are in Your Hands –

We love You Lord - Ron

Cantaloupe

Dear Jesus:

I had never met her yet, as she appeared beside me in all her glory, I knew in an instant all about her. I welcomed the woman of whom John's writings had referred in his fourth chapter, as the Samaritan woman. With a grin she made note of my questioning.

"Before I too crossed through the Gate, I so wondered that even with all the glory of the Heavenly Realm, couldn't one become bored?" Well In a portion of a millisecond 'Glory Time', I have that question answered along with a vast multitude of others." Now, before you join with the Angelic Host before the Throne, may we open your diary. – Appearing before us pre-opened; Ah, yes here it is,

Dear Jesus:

I awoke this morning, well before 5:30. Sleep would not return. Crawling out of bed I dressed, then thought I'd have a look around. Thank you, Jesus, for having me notice a building crane on the top of a building across the street.

I spent the next hour wandering about, taking in the sights and sounds of the early A.M. in our new community. My travel thus far had taken me to a hill-side portion of the city. Then, glancing at my watch realized that Elaine would be up and breakfast waiting. I turned to return our new home. Then realization; where was home? I was completely lost. A brief prayer of "Lord, where am I? Where are You?" then as panic increased, from the top of this hillside, I looked over my surroundings. There off in the distance, I spotted a building crane. "Lord, I asked, is that the same crane. I headed toward the crane and a half hour later was enjoying breakfast. Shortly after breakfast the doorbell chimed. Opening the door, the Yoshizawa's bowed and presented us with an ornate box. "Shall I open?" I asked. Nodding then, "please". Opening the box, I discovered a carefully wrapped cantaloupe. Upon my thanking the Yoshizawa's for their most kind gift, they took their leave. Over the next couple of days we discovered that when back home in Canada, Elaine would pick up a cantaloupe on sale for a dollar (often less) and I'd enjoy it at lunch-time at the office. We must be overlooking something. Then on our first visit to the shopping centre we discovered a cantaloup – Noticed by a clerk, she approached and in halting English. "OH – the king of fruit. A special gift for someone?" Elaine quickly converted the price into Canadian dollars; Seventy-nine dollars! It was apparent we had much to learn.

I love You Lord. Ron

Mamushi

Dear Jesus:

How I hate snakes!' I've always feared those slimy slithering reptiles. I've been repeatedly told that snakes aren't slimy. Maybe so, but please Lord never place me close enough to one to change my opinion. Allow me to go to my grave maintaining that they are slithering slimy creatures. Just the day, before I had stumbled across an article on the Mamushi, Japan's contribution to the reptilian world of nightmares. There it was as clear as clear could be: I read with racing pulse, "There's only one species of poisonous snake indigenous to our area of Japan." Somehow that didn't seem comforting. I could almost see my loving wife clad in black singing the last verse of; Shall We Gather At The River. I read on: "It is about 18 inches long" Small enough to crawl up a missionary's pant leg! "Grayish-brown" Ninety-nine-point nine percent invisible, I cringed, "with a triangular head", I was never good at geometry, but obviously, that's a shape designed for both speed and silent running. Well Lord, You brought us here. We leave the future in your hands.

I Love You Lord – Ron

Communication

Dear Jesus

As I walked along with a Japanese friend, I mentioned my concern about the Mamushi. Yoshizawa was very supportive, but his English limited and my non-existent Japanese didn't give me assurance. Our conversation proceeded;

Qu. Are there poisonous snakes here?

An. - ah yes.

Qu. poisonous snakes?

An. - yes, poisonous snakes.

Qu. Are they dangerous?

An. - Yes, very dangerous, very dangerous.

Qu. Where do they live?

An. where bamboo grows.

Qu. like over there? Ah. - yes there.

Qu. And, are there many poisonous snakes?

An. - many, very dangerous.

Qu. When do the snakes come out.

An. - In the spring.

Well, Lord, the possibility of my worst night mare becoming a reality loomed ominously just around the corner. As I cringed in thought, I recalled a long forgotten verse of scripture;

"For I, the Lord your God, hold your right hand; it is I who say to you, "Fear not, I am the one who helps you." Then I had a 'brilliant' thought. After all my Japanese friend has only a minimal command of the English language, possibly there was a breakdown in communication. Lord, our adventure continues.

I Love You Lord – Ron

Cultural Understanding

Dear Jesus

    I sat down with my Japanese teacher to calmly discuss the situation. "Let's see", she said; "What did Yoshizawa San, say?" "My question was: "Are there poisonous snakes here?" My friend's reply, 'Ah yes' meaning there are poisonous snakes here". "Poisonous snakes"? "Confirmation that you were discussing poisonous snakes. "Are they dangerous?" "Well of course if you find a poisonous snake it's dangerous," "Where do they live?" "Where bamboo grows". "Like over there?" "Well there was bamboo growing over there, snakes live near bamboo so of course, like over there." "They come out in the spring and are dangerous". With, "poisonous snakes, one must be careful, policemen have snake bite serum." Jesus, I thank you for sending us to this land, but Lord, help me to better understand so many things, that I may serve You more fully. A few days would pass, then Elaine's GASP, "Ron, come here" Something was wrong, her voice was filled with fear. She was shaking, trembling. "Ron, I just saw a HUGE SNAKE! It slithered to our gate, then, then up and over the gate without even slowing down. It must have been," Elaine paused; "must have been almost fifteen feet long. We love you Lord, but do we have something to fear, Keep us safe Lord,"

I Love You Lord, Ron

The Immigration Office

Dear Jesus:

We visited the Japanese Immigration office to request an extension for our visiting grandson. The visit of a gaijin 'foreigner' to a government office unfolds as a comic operetta: Mrs. Kikukama, being Japanese, was therefore accomplished with; 'Please, please', and came along, to plead our case. For several minutes, she begged, permission for James to stay another couple of months. She assured them that we, (his Grandparents) were truly honourable people, albeit North Americans. The Immigration officer refused to budge. "NO! IT CAN'T BE DONE." Pressing home, I pointed out that we couldn't get an earlier flight than the one agreed upon between the Consul General in Canada and his parents for him, without great additional cost, again stressing their Consulate in Canada had assured his parents, 'Japan was a friendly country they would have no trouble.' I placed a letter on official stationery, from a friendly Canadian politician, before the officer. Thinking for a moment then said that he must confer with his superior? Stepping behind a screen the officer 'conferred' with his

Ron Hobden

'boss'. From my vantage point, I had an unobstructed view. There wasn't anyone else behind that screen! After a while, (longer than one would usually confer with an invisible supervisor), he advised that ours is a VERY special case. We must apply for special permission. In due course these completed forms were given to another officer. We are again informed 'ours is a very special case. This must be examined very carefully.' Then, that Elaine should go down to the main floor and buy a 4000-yen stamp which is the cost of the extension. My wife returns clutching a 4000-yen stamp and grandson's passport is collected. We thank the officer for the trouble and inconvenience we have caused and leave the office. "Jesus, I thank you for helpful friends like Mrs. Kikukama."

Lord did I mention that prominently displayed in the immigration office is a sign which reads in large bold letters; "Absolutely no Visa extensions granted" … underneath a second line; "Visa extensions 4000 yen". Heavenly Father, each day I 'wrestle' with the norms of this society where You have placed us; For this morning's devotions I turned to the Old Testament to one of Your most amazing servants the prophet Deborah. One of the most amazingly talented people who seemed to be able to do it all. She was a leader, a judge, a prophetess, a wife, and a mother. And along with that, she courageously led her people into battle. Phenomenally inspirational! As Deborah managed, succeeded in her calling, surely with Your leading, I can meet the challenges that appear before me each day.

I Love You Lord – Ron

Elaine's Exhausted

Dear Jesus

Lord, this has been a week filled with tears. Our neighbour at the height of the storm remembered that an upstairs window was not shuttered. Upon opening the window and reaching out for the shutter, a flying roof tile slammed into her. She lost her life. Lord, may the family of our neighbour feel Your love through our care. Then, on this past Sunday we prayed for a young woman whose husband, a diver was killed by a shark.

Lord, I try so hard to communicate Your Gospel to these people and to their loved ones. There is a pain within me that asks "WHY? How could anyone refuse such a precious gift as Your gift of eternal salvation? Lord, help us, guide Your church that we may be empowered to teach and share Your message of salvation and words of love. Lord, we have loved our work for You here. What a blessing You have bestowed upon us. But Lord Elaine is exhausted. Elaine has a weekly lecture at the university. Her weekly preparation time alone exceeds forty hours. We team teach several classes. Yesterday her train travel to waiting students as usual exceeded two

Ron Hobden

hours. Lord, this morning we celebrated a national holiday. All our classes were closed. We slept in a bit Then as we had breakfast, I noticed that Elaine was "as white as a sheet. And trembling. I realized in an instant that our work was to be terminated. We needed to go home to Canada. But Lord as I begin sending notice of our termination to our students, I have no understanding how we can finance a trip home.

I considered sending word home and asking for help, but Elaine said 'First, let's bring this to Jesus." I fully believed that Jesus was fully aware of our situation but at Elaine's motioning we knelt in prayer. I don't know how long we remained in prayer yet as the moments passed so did our apprehension. At the conclusion of our petition, we sensed a feeling of peace. Recalling we had some time ago taught our students That: The Bible tells us that God will make a way where there seems to be no other way. We prayed for strength for our next few days.

The next couple of days were strange to us. Both without students, I watched so pleased as I saw (or imagined) slight improvement. Yet a determination that we were doing the right thing in resigning our teaching and preparing for a trip home – A trip home yet beyond our financial ability. Somehow while we had advised our students that due to Elaine's illness it was time for us to sadly resign but somehow, we were not to advise of our financial need. The following day I received a phone call from one of my students. Could we meet her at McDonalds Restaurant?

As we enjoyed many cups of coffee at "Macdonaldos" I agreed. An hour passed then as we entered the restaurant, I noticed Mikiko's wave. We had a cup of coffee with scarcely a word or two exchanged. Finishing her coffee, Mikiko stood, reached into her purse and with- drew an envelope. "Pastor, please don't open this until you are back at home" and quickly made her way out of the restaurant.

Arriving home we opened the envelope. A note saying that God told her to give this to us. In the envelope we counted seven thousand American dollars. We wept for a few moments then Elaine opened her Bible to Psalm 91

> *Because he holds fast to me in love, I will deliver him; I will protect him, because he knows my name. When he calls to me, I will answer him; I will be with him in trouble; I will rescue him and honor him. With long life I will satisfy him and show him my salvation.*

As we marvelled at our creator's words we felt His message to us; "Well done" intertwined with; "As you cling to Me, so shall I cling to you."

I Love You Lord - Ron

What is Truth

Dear Jesus:

A few wonderfully blessed years have passed since our graduation from Bible College. My doctrinal thesis completed; I now await a decision from the university council. For three years I have been searching for an answer to the question; "What Is Truth"? For five years I was a police officer. For seven years a Justice of the Peace. For forty years a pastor.

In all that time, I searched for a definitive answer to the question, 'WHAT IS TRUTH?" During the time I served with the Department of Justice, I attended hundreds of cases in court. I listened to men and women; many devoted Christians of absolute integrity. For them to tell, an 'untruth', was unthinkable, yet their versions, their testimony of what happened, was filled with contradictory inaccuracies. One witness would say the man who robbed the store was a teenager, another would say he was middle aged. One would swear he had long blond hair, another that he had short black hair. Yet, I perceived each was telling 'the truth'. The deeper I studied into Holy Writ, and works of secular authors one point remained constant: The truth is still the truth even if no one believes it. A lie is still a lie, even if everyone believes it. Troubled, I turned to my Bible. In James 2:25, Rahab the prostitute, is called righteous because she deceived. Because she lied, she is righteous?

I turned to the Old Testament to the story of Abraham and read:

> *"Now there was a famine in the land, and Abram went down to Egypt to live there for a while because the famine was severe. As he was about to enter Egypt, he said to his wife Sarai, "I know what a beautiful woman you are. When the Egyptians see you, they will say, 'This is his wife.' Then they will kill me but will let you live. Say you are my sister, so that I will be treated well for your sake and my life will be spared because of you."*
> Genesis 12:10-13

Then I consulted John 16:13; "But when the Spirit of truth, comes, he will guide you into all truth". This seemed clear enough: But scripture also labels numerous persons who intentionally told inaccuracies, lies, were deceivers, as blessed. "Lord, I need clarification if I am ever to submit this thesis." Then sitting at my desk, my open Bible before me, I read of my Lord's arrest in the Garden; The soldier's question; "Are you Jesus of Nazareth?" And Jesus said, "I am" But wait! I questioned; According to Jewish law, one was always from the country, community where they were born. True, He had grown up in Nazareth, but; The

Bethlehem manger; Legally he was a Bethlehemite. How could he have been truthful?

I knew my Lord was without sin, how might this be resolved? The hour was late. At Elaine's urging, I went to bed. In the morning as I awoke, with clarity, I reasoned: Truth therefore, is ANYTHING, which conforms to the known or unknown will of God.

Truth MAY on occasion employ deceit, manipulation or distortion to achieve certain desired goals. Almost two thousand years ago, Truth was put on trial and judged by people who were devoted to lies. In fact, Truth faced six trials in less than one full day, three of which were religious, and three that were legal. In the end, few people involved in those events could answer the question, "What is truth?

There is only one absolute test to determine 'truth'. **Does it conform to BOTH the known and unknown will of God**? If the conclusion of that test is positive, whatever the circumstance may be; IT IS TRUTH.

As I submitted my thesis, I offered thanks to my Lord. Now I await the answer.

I Love You Lord – Ron

Doctor Hobden

Dear Jesus:

In my hand, I hold my diploma; "Ronald David Hobden - Doctor of Science in Theology." How unlikely, how unrealistic this moment. As a high school dropout after barely completing grade ten. Elaine's mother had a friend, Mr. Purdy, who was principal of a High School an hour's drive to the west. Upon Elaine's mom voicing her concerns about my future as a high school drop-out, Mr. Purdy, offered me the opportunity of enrolling in Blind River High. I was astonished. Through the 'generosity of my teachers, I was given a bare passing mark for grade ten. NOW Mr. Purdy's suggesting that I resume studies. As I recall Mr. Purdy was quite persuasive and Elaine's mother wouldn't take 'NO' for an answer.

Arriving Monday morning, I was ushered into Principal Purdy's office by a staff member. "Mr. Hobden" after discussing your case with my staff, it has been decided to place you on probation in grade thirteen. "Mr. Purdy, Did you look at my report from Massey High? Do you know that the only reason that I was given a passing grade was that I had stated my intention to drop out?" Mr. Purdy nodded then continued; "I called Principal Cassie, one of your former teachers, he assures me that in his opinion, had you put an effort into your studies you would succeed. I want you to accept the challenge of grade thirteen for one month". The month passed, then called into the principal's office, I was greeted with; "Mr. Hobden, I feel that you are wasting your time here with us." "But Mr. Purdy, this is what I have been saying from the beginning." "No, son, when I say that you are wasting your time here, that's not it at all. I have made arrangements for you to write a university entrance exam, at Laurentian University in Sudbury. There is an appointment for you this Wednesday afternoon at 1:30 p.m. I believe that there's an interesting future ahead for you. Take care." In a state of shock, I took his outstretched hand and made my way out to my car then headed home.

Arriving at Laurentian, I was ushered into an office, met by the principal then turned over to a professor who explained the procedure; "This is a five-hour series of what we call 'questionaries' spread over two days. As luck has it we have openings for you at 9:15 tomorrow and Friday mornings. The tests were not at all as I had anticipated. Seemed to be focused upon, general knowledge, and understanding of single words or sentences and a few items featured on the evening national news. I had some concern when on both days, I completed the tests well under the allotted time; was I missing something? The dean of students introduced himself then confirmed that I was finished. As I collected my papers he asked if I could come back Monday afternoon. With the arrival of Monday afternoon as directed, I sat in the library awaiting my 'fate'. Both the principal and dean of students appeared. With a smile, the dean broke the silence; "Mr. Hobden, well done! we are pleased to welcome you to Laurentian as a mature student. You are invited to take on two subjects. Upon satisfactory completion of those two courses, to carry a full load of classes leading toward your bachelor's degree. Thus it was that after just one year at Laurentian, and a further two years at Aldersgate and awarded some credit for: graduation from Police College, my pilot's license and miscellaneous studies, I held in my hand a bachelor's degree, paving the way, paving the way later for a masters and finally my PhD. It was a long and at times a frustrating journey. Lord, you have led Elaine and me along amazing paths. We have learned that when we listen to your leading nothing is impossible.

The fax came in the middle of the night. Our daughter was at the hospital about to have a baby. We had been anticipating this little one's birth for months and the child was finally coming! It would be months before we got to meet this new addition to our clan. I so wished to be there to meet our grandchild, but Japan was many thousands of miles away! I was to miss out on a lot of moments like this one. I must admit a tear trickled down my manly face as I boarded the train this morning. Later a touch of the Saviour's love enriched my soul. That evening I opened my diary for another entry

I Love You Lord – Ron

My Open Diary

Ibaraki, my spirit guide approached, "There are many events in your diary. Now consider your pages, early in your ministry;" Your diary has already appeared at your side and opened to the appropriate passage.

Dear Jesus:

Lord, I'm at my wits end! How do I reach these people?" Mockingly they question; how dare I go around proclaiming that I know the one and only way?" In our modern culture, there are many who attempt to make the followers of Jesus seem arrogant and prideful causing more and more "modern people" to view the Church in an increasingly harsh light. Cleverly these false messengers teach that evangelism can best be served by a living witness, but by doing so they make a mockery of the redemption of the Cross.

My Bible proclaims a day the time of which no one knows, not even the angels in heaven, nor the Son, but only the Father. Then it seemed that I heard Him say – "Stand tall you are being tested. Heed the word of one of my hymn writers.

Guide me, O thou great Jehovah,
pilgrim though this barren land;
I am weak, but thou art mighty;
hold me with thy powerful hand;
Bread of heaven, Bread of heaven
feed me now and evermore

I love You Lord – Ron

A God In The Forest

Dear Jesus:

You have placed us in this land of eight million gods. Lord, we are so astonished as we are confronted with the myriad of deities to which these people bow. Our astonishment peeked last Saturday afternoon as we were walking along a trail in a forested area of one of the many parks. We came to a clearing, where what we saw was difficult to comprehend. It must be a god, but - ? We'd come across many local deities, all placed upon firm footings. Animals, insects, planetary objects, fire gods, the sun, moon, star gods. Goddess of the dawn, the list was endless but here before our eyes something over two meters tall, – It looked like a – Elaine commented, "It is!" It's part of the male anatomy!" Hearing someone approaching, we quickly moved away. Looking back from a distance. We watched briefly as a young woman, bowed in prayer before this 'god'. Heavenly Father, help us to make Your presence known in this land. O Lord, among the gods there is none like you, O Lord -Of all those worshipped as gods there is no one that can hear, and none which can save. Lord, thank you that I have a God who can hear; while these gods are silent and voiceless. O Lord guide us into how to teach that You are the One to whom one may always come;

I love You Lord – Ron

A Home For A God

Dear Jesus

The workmen were feverishly, putting the final touches on Amaterasu's new home. It is nothing elaborate since she has a new home built for her every twenty years. Actual construction began forty years ago when workmen planted the trees that provide today's lumber for Amaterau's latest home. It's not that the old residence is beyond repair, it's just that the mistress decreed that she shall have a new dwelling every twenty years. She's been doing so for the past twelve hundred and twenty years. Actually, Amaterua's been 'residing' on the present site since 4 BC. Amaterua is the sun goddess. She's revered as the ancestral goddess of Japan's Imperial family and guardian of the nation. Every year about six million people visit her home.

When all is ready, Shinto priests will don their white robes and lend a helping hand with moving arrangements. As each Emperor ascends the throne, he MUST make a pilgrimage to Ise, to personally convey the good news. Sometime in early June, the crown prince will arrive at her door shortly after his marriage, to relay the news of his wedding. Lord, I need Your guidance. Oh Lord, how do I teach that You commanded we Christians to love You with all of our heart, all our soul all our strength, and all our mind.

I Love You Lord – Ron

Ron Hobden

It's Just A Baby

Dear Jesus:

I was upstairs when the house began to shake. It lasted only for a few seconds, but was an interesting experience to say the least. The paper reported it to be a THREE on the Richter scale so it was 'just a baby.' As the house started to shake, Elaine called upstairs and asked what I'd done. Now while I will accept the responsibility for a fau paux or two, however I go on the offensive, when accused of causing an earthquake! Actually, we had one the day before and the day after but they were so small, they escaped our attention. A couple of days ago, an earthquake out in the ocean caused tidal waves, putting the police, and fire department on the alert as the military monitored their path towards Japan. There were many warnings on the TV about the coming tidal waves.

Lord help me to convey to these people that when they bring these concerns to the Lord then listen for and follow instructions, Yes, they walk in anxiety, they are not walking in faith. Lord, they want to be men and women of faith, yet often worry becomes their middle name. We're familiar with the small trickle of fear that meanders through our minds until it cuts a channel into which all other thoughts are drained. Lord, help me to help them place their anxiety upon You.

I Love You Lord, Ron

Ron Hobden

Miyago – On Duty

Dear Jesus

I can sleep through police sirens, thunderstorms, even a mild tremor or two, however, not even Rip Van Winkle could make it through the night when Miyago's on duty. During last night's nocturnal patrols, she detected an unpleasant odour in the kitchen. She jumped on the bed dashed across my face, then tore down stairs, then upstairs and across our bed again then down stairs, and repeated the procedure three or four times. It took some time for me to decided I'd better investigate just what was going on in the lower level. Part way down the stairs, the smell of natural gas was overpowering. Had she not wakened me and had the fridge motor kicked in, Elaine and I might well have been the first Canadian pastors in space. Thank You Lord, we have Your word.

"The LORD will keep you from all harm—
he will watch over your life; the LORD will

watch over your coming and going both now and forevermore" Psalm 121:7-8

Thank You for giving Miyago to us. Thank you for Your ever vigilant watch over us.
I Love You Lord - Ron

Miyago On Patrol

Dear Jesus

Once before Miyago had wakened me in the middle of the night, and in the early hours of the morning, she sounded the alarm once more.

As my weary eyes came into focus the sight of a scorpion a foot away from my face was a sight to behold. Is that a CAT, or is that a CAT??

Now, in Japan, it's cultural to thank anyone, usually with a gift, for every good deed. It only seemed appropriate to reward Miyago, but what does one offer a cat? We thought this one over then went out shopping and bought her a package of shrimp. Later when we sat down to supper, Elaine placed a plate of shrimp before Miyago. She approached this new delicacy, backed away, approached it, then caught another scent; my chicken. What could I do? Here's this feline, standing on her hind feet reaching up and patting me, Oh well, I did save a piece of the tender juicy bird for myself, a small piece! Lord, in true Japanese form, this humble Canadian thanks You for Miyago and for the words from today's devotional from.

> The LORD will keep you from all harm—
> he will watch over your life. Psalm 121:7

I Love You Lord, Ron

Thanksgiving Shopping

Dear Jesus:

Back in September, we ordered both our Thanksgiving and Christmas turkeys. The Thanksgiving bird has arrived and we have high hopes for December's order. As no respectable Thanksgiving table sans cranberries is complete, we resigned ourselves to making the trek to an International Store in the port city of Kobe.

Arriving in Kobe, we had some difficulty getting our bearings. It had been nearly four years since we had last visited Kobe Grocers. That was before the Hanshin earthquake.

Profound sadness gripped us as we passed by a new high rise. It was on this site that one of our friends perished in the quake. We walked for nearly an hour crisscrossing the area without locating Kobe Grocers

Deciding that it was pointless to continue our quest, we decided to return to the station. Suddenly, there it was! Kobe Grocers. Our favourite food source had survived the quake! After thirty minutes shopping, our back packs were heavy as we left the store, cans of cranberries, pumpkin pie filling, even Crest toothpaste! And other numerous treasured edibles. Lord as we remember those who lost family and friends, may our service this Sunday express the joy and the praise of those who love You

I Love You Lord – Ron

Where is Golden B.C.?

Dear Jesus

The fax 'beep' resounded. And so it was, we learned we were ordered back to Canada. We had petitioned to stay. Later we would learn the deceitfulness of our superintendent. Now, where is Golden British Columbia? Memories of the past two years in this exotic land flashed before my eyes. So many friends, so many sights. We were leaving a growing church, what would become of the faithful band that so enthusiastically greeted us each Sunday?

My highway map of western Canada reveals our new posting, Golden, B.C., to be situated only 166 kilometres west of Banff. Mountains, hot springs, mountain air, scenery such as only Your mighty hand can sculpt! Yet, as Elaine and I will soon walk the streets of 'Golden' I suspect, there will be memory twinges as we reminisce on kimono clad ladies, wild flowers in January, sushi, shark fin soup, raw beef, cold octopus...! As we questioned this move, we recalled words from John; "You did not choose Me, but I chose you. (John 15:16)" You did not choose Me, but I chose you and appointed you that you should go and bear fruit" As we mulled over those words, we kept going back to; "that you should go." Well Lord, wherever you place us, that's okay.

I Love You Lord, Ron

Women - Saved Through Childbearing

Dear Jesus:

Lord, as we settle in here in Golden how are we to deal with this new betrayal? This evening, the board was surprised to hear that Elaine was planning to serve as pastor. They had met with the superintendent and voiced their disapproval of a female behind their pulpit. He had advised that he'd deal with it, that it wouldn't be a problem. Yet there was not even a hint in all our communication, written or verbal of the matter. Explaining our stand on this issue, together with ample proof from God's Word, I turned to an adamant member and quoted:

> *"For God so loved the world that he gave his one and only Son, that whoever believes in him shall not perish but have eternal life."*
> *John 3:16*

Then asked if he was in agreement with this text. "Pastor, he muttered, "This church knows, that is the only way to salvation." "Is this for everyone," I countered. Everyone spoke out or confirmed by nodding. Then I cautioned, "but this surely applies only to we men. Would you please stand and read 1Timothy 2:15. Somehow, he'd missed recalling this text. Standing, he flipped open his Bible and began;

> *"But women will be saved through childbearing - if they continue in faith, love and holiness with propriety.*

"So, if it is your contention that scripture is to be accepted without question, do you invoke John's teaching and deny Timothy's? As we step out, may I remind you that as Elaine, an ordained pastor, has given birth to six children and has also embraced John 3:16 that she has met BOTH requirements of God's Word. I would also suggest that when this comes to a vote that it be done by ballot, allowing each of you to respond according to your heart and without pressure. There was complete silence as we left the room. Twenty minutes later our presence was requested. I noticed that there were two empty chairs. The chairman's comments seemed to echo a sigh of relief.

The ballots were counted, it was six to two in favour of a request that we remain as pastors. There had been a division in the board for years as to female preachers. Most of the congregation were hesitant to stand against the two families in the church. While they would miss the two dissenting families, some believed that these 'archaic' attitudes were the cause of their dwindling congregation.

One of the elders rose from his seat, and quoted the slightly adjusted words of a hymn.

Pastors Ron AND Pastor Elaine; We sing because we're happy, We sing because we're free. For His eye is on the sparrow, And we know He watches us. At his motion the congregation joined in.

I love You Lord – Ron

Failed Leadership

Dear Jesus:

The folk accepted Elaine as their pastor. We now feel comfortable in Golden. We might continue here until retirement. We purchased an acreage a few miles out of the community. In response to my service in the military, having served previously as Royal Canadian padre, I was asked to once again take on the office of Chaplaincy at Golden. But Lord, I have received devastating news this week. One of our leaders was discovered having inappropriate conduct with a teen. It is under investigation and the police have advised that I must keep the information that has come to me confidential. It cannot be made known prior to a trial. Informing our bishop, I was instructed that until the matter is resolved before the court, the accused must be barred from all leadership within the church's ministry

Following the bishop's instructions, I gave each board member a copy of the bishop's fax, waited for a few moments for them to absorb the content then read the bishop's fax to the congregation. Several demanded answers to matters which I was not at liberty to divulge, whereupon a third of

Ron Hobden

the gathering walked out. Lord, only you know how this is going to end. Lord we need, I need your guidance and assurance. Lord help us, help your church.

I love You Lord – Ron

Retirement At Last

Dear Jesus:

We are trusting that this move is acceptable to you; Months ago after tendering our resignation, we purchased a large trailer and a truck to haul it and signed on with M.A.P.S, a volunteer organization of Christian campers. Our first appointment has been at a boy's ranch in Florida. They have provided hook-ups for our trailer as we offered our services to the Ranch. I was asked to serve as chapel leader, each morning leading the devotions.

Most days, I worked at various assignments while Elaine was assigned to the camp office. So it was that during the summer months we worked at a church camp in Canada and were now into our second year. Then after two months we were asked if we would accept teaching high school positions at a Boys Camp some distance up north. With apprehension and prayer, we headed for this new challenge. The first few days went cautiously well. By cautious, I mean that our students being wards of the court were to be kept under close observation. They were subject to sudden fits of temper. Teachers had to always be on the lookout for violent outbursts. By the third day it became obvious that our students had learned to manipulate the system. They soon discovered and passed their findings on to the student body. Attendance at Sunday worship was mandatory. Wednesday prayer was voluntary.

If they came home after service 'speaking in tongues' they were rewarded for the week. By our third week I was asked by the director if I spoke in tongues. At my answer in the negative, he mentioned that if I quietly mouthed the words 'bow ties and dirty socks" it would pass. That afternoon, we packed and began our journey home to Canada. That evening as we went before You Lord in prayer we recalled; Lord thank you for having Paul enlightening us through Your Word. Their work will be shown for what it is, because the Day will bring it to light. It will be revealed with fire, and the fire will test the quality of each person's work. If what has been built survives, the builder will receive a reward. If it is burned up, the builder will suffer loss but yet will be saved—even though only as one escaping through the flames. (1 Corinthians 3:13-16) Lord may our departure from the assignment cause the staff to search your holy scripture that their concept of worship be Your concept of worship.

> *Show us your ways, LORD, teach us your paths. Guide us in your truth and teach us, for you are God our Saviour, and our hope is in you all day long.*

We love You Lord – Ron

An Invitation

Dear Jesus:

We had settled in for a quiet evening when the telephone interrupted the silence. It was our friend Sara, a British consul general calling from London England. "Ron, if Elaine's there, can you put me on speaker?" "Go ahead Sarah she's here." "Hi, I have a bit of a dilemma. I've been asked to assist a couple of hundred Japanese students who wish to begin a Japanese speaking church in Edinburgh. We have a church here who is enthusiastically offering support, but lacking the organizational skills they are hesitant in commencing. I have an idea; Could you two consider coming over and conducting a church leadership seminar, say for about a week?" They would cover all your costs and you are welcome to stay with pastors Stephan and Yuki. Then, I was thinking if you could make it a two-week stint, I'd love to have you stay with me. Be wonderful to bring each other up to date."

How could we turn down such a proposal! So it was, that later in the month, what a privilege on Sunday afternoon to stand today before a congregation of Japanese brothers and sisters at St Barnabas Church, London. The exciting days passed so quickly. At the conclusion of our time, and with our seminar concluded, "Lord may our contribution in the past weeks bear fruit for Your kingdom."

I love You – Lord - Ron

Japan Calling

Dear Jesus

Two years of our 'retirement' have passed, we are sensing your calling us to return to Japan. Time to put our affairs in order. We have enjoyed these two years on our 'retirement' acreage. Our home nestled on the side of a majestic mountain. Many visitors have said in awe that we had a 'million-dollar view' from our living room window. Yet with heavy hearts we put our 'treasure' our home, on the market. It was soon sold and we received from the sale sufficient to meet our needs of travel and support for our adjustment to Japan.

Lord, as we question this move, we recall our motivation for our first tour in Japan, as today we questioned, as we recalled the Sunday evening when we received the request leading to Japan. There wasn't the slightest thought in our minds yet for some unknown reason (at the time) as the service closed, Elaine once again, felt led to change our closing hymn in favour of; Mary Brown's hymn; 'I'll Go

Where You Want Me To Go Dear Lord"; then that evening came the call, 'We want you to come to Japan."

With a slight tear trickling down her cheek, Elaine's nod was my assurance that we were to return to the Land of the rising SON.

Return to the Land of the Rising SON

Dear Jesus:

Was this flight back to the Land of the Rising SON a hint of things to come? First, we were an hour late departing from Edmonton due to heavy thunderstorms. Then there would be a brief delay due to a problem in the aircraft's navigational computer. At midpoint of the second hour, I suggested to a stewardess, that all the pilot had to do was point the plane in the right direction for ten hours then land. Smiling she whispered in my ear that while my theory was sound, if Kansai's runway failed to appear in the captain's window before we ran out of fuel, any of a thousand great white sharks would find me tasty. After those words of wisdom, another two- and one-half hours passed before the pilot's authoritative voice advised that they had cancelled the flight, ordered busses and at company's expense would "put us up in a very ritzy hotel, then pick us up next morning at 5:30 am. for a 7:00 am departure." After a delicious evening meal, a comfortable bed, our bus arrived on time and Air

Canada # 891 finally got off at 7:30 a.m. Ten hours later touched down at Kansai airport. Thus, we returned to the land of the rising "Son" where You have called us to serve for however long?

I Love You Lord - Ron

The Rolls-Royce Tradition

Dear Jesus:

It's Easter Sunday Lord! May there be an expectation in our hearts and the heart of our congregation of that miracle of the first Easter. The service was a blessing. I felt especially touched as a stranger entered the church. I had not met him before, but took notice that he had a speech impediment and communicated by a horse whisper and hand gestures. It was obvious that he was well known in the congregation. Watanabi san introduced me to the stranger and my initial suspicion of inebriation was quickly absolved. His command of English and use of a writing tablet more than adequate for conversation. Noting his attire, and assuming that he was most likely a homeless man, I motioned to Watanabi and suggested that since our congregation had a tradition of having an after-church meal in a restaurant that I'd be pleased to cover the costs of his meal.

Watanabi just smiled then said. Pastor, you spoke of traditions in your sermon this afternoon. I must tell you that here in this church, we also have a tradition, Anyone who drives to church in a new Rolls-Royce buys his own meal!

This man is a deaf multimillionaire. Holy Spirit, guide us in this land that we may see the nuances of strangers who come to worship.

I Love You Lord – Ron

'God' Shops

Dear Jesus:

On a walk through a mall this afternoon we came across a 'god shop'. That's what foreigners call the shops that sell all manner of 'worship' paraphernalia. One can purchase (or order) items ranging from 3 cm to 3-meter statutes of their favourite god and almost countless butstats, which is a shelter for one's god.

They usually contain an array of subsidiary religious accessories such as: candlesticks, incense burners, bells, and platforms for placing offerings such as fruit, tea or rice, and also urns containing the cremated remains of relatives. Then to cover all 'bases' there are: emerald crosses, necklaces, enamel or silver crucifixes and pictures of 'Jesus'. Traditional Japanese beliefs associate the Butstat to be a house of the Buddha, as well as deceased relatives they enshrine within it. The price of a Butstat can vary differently In Japan. A typical one ranges between $150.00 to $5000.00 US dollars. In 2008 someone paid $630,000 for a special order..

Ron Hobden

While I am assured it is Your will to have a transformation from the six million gods to the ONE true God of all creation, Lord help me to embrace Your leading in this land.

I Love You Lord - Ron

Japanese Honour

Dear Jesus

Here, honour is everything! When there is a proposal of marriage, parents, usually mothers, visit city hall, if there is a police record for even the slightest matter, there is a loss of honour. The wedding will not take place. Here, honour is everything. Lord, I so need Your help to teach that Jesus is the epitome of honour.

I Love You Lord - Ron

Ibarashi interjected; "now as the years have passed during this perhaps your final visit. Recall an entry in your diary as you struggled to present Jesus to your people. You wrote: Dear Jesus: I am having great difficulty explaining Your message of 'forgiveness'. I have discovered that here in Japan, honour is everything. Imbedded in Japanese psyche is that without honour one is unworthy of being in society. While so-called 'white collar crime' is admitted, theft, is virtually unknown.

I have a ritual when family or friends from Canada visit. Sometime during the afternoon, I clothespin a 1000-yen bill (ten dollars Canadian) on my gate, in full view of thousands of passers-by. My visiting family knowing how minimal my wage is, are shocked when I leave the bill on the gate and walk away. They are even more shocked the next morning when my thousand yen note is still there. Thousands of people passed by my gate, with my bill in full view. I suggested that they try that back home. Then I finish the matter by showing a copy of The Japan Times. On the front page, a bicycle stolen from the university parking lot. My people question: "Pastor, you say I need 'forgiveness'? I never lie, steal, I'm an honourable person, I NEED FORGIVNESS?

With deep concern. – How do I reach these people Lord? I took the problem to Jesus: Now, you recall awakening in the morning with one word affixed in your memory. What was that word?" Miracles: and your next sermon touched many hearts as you spoke of one of God's hallmarks is that He heals people, who can't be helped by medical treatment. Of Jesus performing thousands of miraculous healings and His command that those who believe in Him were to do the same. That was the beginning of our ministry to these people."

Thank you Jesus! Now as the time has passed and once again, we are homeward bound and really heading into retirement, we have said our farewells. In less than an hour our ride to Kansai Airport will pick us up. In less than fourteen hours we shall land in Vancouver then to Edmonton and the bus to Lloydminster. Kevin a car salesman whom we have never met, will pick us up in a van we have purchased from him sight unseen. Then on to our new home in Chauvin, Alberta. (Well Lord, new to us). Again thankyou that our friends from the church checked out the house and property. Sent us all the information and photos. Then two ladies from the church went and a second exam from a woman's point of view. These kinds trusting folk after receiving our reply to their view then dropping in on the real estate office about the house and their affirmation, our friend the realtor even personally paid a deposit to hold the house for us. Thank you, Lord, for the wonderful ten years of service You permitted us to have in this great land. But we are excited about being back to our homeland. We don't know what this retirement means but Lord we are in Your hands.

Our taxi to the airport shall arrive within the next few minutes. Past memories flood my soul. Earthquakes, typhoons, highlights over the past years, our feeding program for the homeless that mushroomed from forty meals once a week to thousands twice each week. My thoughts are interrupted by the telephone; it was one of our volunteer workers. "Ron, is your T.V. on? Are you watching the news? The demonstration at city hall?"

I had to admit that it was news to me. "It was reported that over a thousand made their way to City Hall to petition for greater support for the feeding program. AND Ron, when the mayor came out to meet with the crowd, their spokesman said; "Hobden Sensei had given them courage to gather to assemble there at city hall." There was a lump in my throat. I had no recollection of this intended gathering, nor had I ever suggested such action. Might I be in trouble? "Pastor Ron, the mayor and his colleagues offered great praise for your efforts." "REALLY," "YES – really. The mayor on hearing that you were leaving said that you will be greatly missed."

Arriving at the airport, we were surrounded by perhaps, twenty-five (or more) parishioners. A farewell that would remain forever in my memory. The flight to Vancouver was uneventful, a ninety-minute pause, then transit to the Edmonton flight. I had arrived in my homeland. Lord what awaits us I questioned as my questioning deepened; anxiety grew. "Lord, what now! As my uneasiness deepened, I recalled the words of a devotional I'd recently read. Words of a troubled writer;

> "I the LORD am your shepherd; You shall
> not want. I shall lead you to green pastures:
> I shall lead you beside the still waters of life.
> Psalm 23

A profound joy filled my heart as I stood among the angelic choir. Back in my younger years, as young pastor my favourite Gospel singers were: Reverend Gary Davis, Thomas A Dorsey, Hank Williams, Mahalia Jackson, Tennessee Ernie Ford and a host of others who brought joy to my heart. Yet all their sacred gifts of music were exceeded a thousand-fold by the angels before the throne. One never grows tired of the never-ending choir appearing at the foot of the Golden Throne. Each song of praise more thrilling than the one preceding. You knew without question that every voice a thousand years into the future shall surpass the preceding.

My guardian had slipped away from a walk along Glory's golden streets to offer his praise for the record I kept in my diary. "How blessed was your praise. Yet it would have become even more blessed if your writing had dwelt more upon your writing of the King's Hand upon your life. Consider: prior to my arrival to escort you to judgement then my walk with you through the Gate. I refer to one of the hymns that so touched your soul.

> *My name is graven on his hands,*
> *my name is written on his heart.*
> *I know that while in heav'n he stands*
> *no tongue can bid me thence depart,*
> *no tongue can bid me thence depart*

Ibarashi declared: – That hymn renewed your will to once again come out of retirement. Note your diary: The print from my diary leapt from entering retirement or entering a new opportunity?" Lord, Elaine and I understand that our ages for 'normal' people place us into the retirement mode. Yet, you have created us some distance from whatever 'normal' might be. Is this an opportunity for a new ministry. Lord Is this where we settle down in our golden years. OR Do You have plans for us?

I Love You Lord – Ron

Lutheran Church Request

Dear Jesus;

We are home for retirement! As I Look back over our years of service and question our future, is there a smile on Your face as You are fully aware of what our future holds.

The first week of our retirement passed by without incident. Then we received a phone call from someone on the church council of the Wainwright/Irma Lutheran church. Could we please meet with them? The meeting was set for Thursday evening. Following a brief devotional. The chairman then answered the question. "We are in the process of calling a pastor, but that will take a couple of months, would you folks consider filling until the arrival of our new pastor." I questioned, "This evening was the first time we have ever been in a Lutheran church. Would our theology our doctrine be acceptable? We have been serving an international church in Japan which has a two-part creed. First, to preach, teach Jesus as personal saviour; second: to live one's life in accordance to the holy scripture,"

From the lips of an elderly member of the board came a resounding "AMEN". Lord, it was that 'amen' that opened the way for our acceptance. Lord, we have no idea what these next couple of months will bring.

I love You Lord – Ron

Ron Hobden

My Beautiful Shirt

Dear Jesus:

By our second day of travel, the scenery as always, was a breath-taking reminder of the majesty of our Creator. Arriving at Banff we set up camp then, noting the time, decided that a trip to the Hot Springs was in order. As this was a special occasion I had packed "The Shirt". The shirt was the culmination of several hours of Elaine's loving labour. So carefully she had matched the pattern as she sewed it together. I had worn it only a couple of times and had always received nods and words of approval. After a relaxing soak, it was time to head back to our campsite. But first a stop at the men's room. As I washed my hands, I observed a middle-aged man that while looking at my shirt seemed to be gazing into my eyes. Determining that my shirt was an advertisement, I was 'propositioned'.

Before I had an opportunity to share my faith, I found myself throwing up. As I cleaned up, I knew that I could never wear that shirt again. Fortunately we were in a swimming area where no one would notice if I walked shirtless from the washroom to our campsite, I removed my most prized shirt and as he stood in silence, I buried it in a garbage receptacle. Lord, did my moment of revulsion cause me to miss an opportunity of reaching out to this lost soul?

I love You Lord – Ron

Thirteen Years of Service

Dear Jesus:

I took a deep breath and said; "Now we don't know a great deal about Lutheran distinctives. For our ministry, we teach preach and live that salvation comes through an acceptance of Jesus Christ as personal Saviour. We attempt to live according to the teachings of Holy Scripture. When one of the elderly ladies across the table from us said; "AMEN' THAT sealed it!

Well Lord, that meeting with the Lutheran church board was to last thirteen years. Only You knew what was ahead as the Wainwright Council Chair presented us with a Christmas gift, concluding his presentation by saying, "Well you two have truly blessed us for the last ten years, Don't you even consider leaving us for another ten years". Quite a remark considering we were rapidly approaching our eighties. Then from your heart you shared; "It has been our joy and honour to serve you this last decade. We shall claim the Lord's blessing of; Luke 12:31 "Seek the Kingdom of God above all else, and he will give you everything you need."

Guide me, O thou great Redeemer,
pilgrim though this barren land;
I am weak, but thou art mighty;
hold me with thy powerful hand

I love You Lord – Ron

Ron Hobden

The Town Drunk

A welcome 'shimmer' "George, I was just reminiscing about you." "Ahh Pastor, I knew that you had arrived, It was you who introduced me to the Saviour. LOOK it's all here:

Dear Jesus

During lunch the phone rang. Lord, forgive me for being annoyed with the interruption but It's been a heavy morning. Clients to see at the hospital. Two appointments at the office and both running late. I was hoping for some solitude by noon. But the phone rang. It was George the 'used to be' town drunk'.

Over thirty years have now passed since that night. When in a drunken stupor he gave his life to You Lord. In an instant, You changed a town drunk into a probation officer to become Your hands in often desperate situations. I recall that years before I was admitted into Glory our Youth Secretary visited the Corps.. The major was noted for his abruptness. George, now a passionate, but calm witness for the Lord, had endured the Major's rudeness long enough. "Major," George commented, "I think you need a conversional experience." The Major attempted to reply but for the moment was lost for words. Lord, you knew I was annoyed when the phone rang. Thank you for this lesson, maybe next time, I'll have learned to keep my emotions in check.

I love You Lord, Ron

A HOT Topic

Dear Jesus:

I was recalling words from 2 Peter 3: advising that the Day of the Lord will come like a thief in the night. An angel has told me that while neither he nor any of the heavenly host, save for the Father, know when the End of the World will happen it will occur suddenly and quickly. Now the end of the world has been a hot topic even to ages past. Some people are preparing for the end of the world with safe houses and food storage shelters. While Paul instructed by the Holy Spirit, tells us the rapture will happen quicker than a twinkling of the eye,

> *I declare to you, brothers and sisters, that flesh and blood cannot inherit the kingdom of God, nor does the perishable inherit the imperishable. Listen, I tell you a mystery: We will not all sleep, but we will all be changed— in a flash, in the twinkling of an eye, at the last trumpet. For the trumpet will sound, the dead will be raised imperishable, and we will*

be changed. For the perishable must clothe itself with the imperishable, and the mortal with immortality. When the perishable has been clothed with the imperishable, and the mortal with immortality, then the saying that is written will come true: "Death has been swallowed up in victory."
(1 Corinthians 15:50-54.)

Lord I pray, help our generation to prepare according to Your leading.

I love You Lord - Ron

Gender Issues

Appearing at my side the great Dr. Martin Luther King Jr. "Ron" He asserted; I found your writing on human decency interesting. Shall we review it again." With that, my diary reopened

Dear Jesus:

You blessed our ministry in this parish. Elaine and I have felt your hand upon us during both joyful and sad moments. I especially thank You for Your leading as we confronted challenges to Your church's proclamation of the saving Word. Here in Glory you review the blessings you received from your standing firm in your living and teaching as the question of 'gender' was raised. It was with deep concern as you opened your Bible to 1 Corinthians 6:9

> *Do you not know that the unrighteous will not inherit the kingdom of God? Do not be deceived. Neither fornicators, nor idolaters, nor adulterers, nor homosexuals, nor sodomites*

Sadly, the man in my office, a member of the church council could see the meaning of the instruction, YET his love for his brother who was emotionally involved with a male, blinded him to the consequences his sibling would one day face. He resigned from council and left us. Lord guide him into Your truth.

I Love You Lord - Ron

Crimes Against Humanity

Dear Jesus:

Give this church the wisdom to teach Your design for the sanctity of holy matrimony.

Dr. King continued; "Indeed, were I still alive today, and when judged against today's empty, politically correct standards, I would no doubt be perpetually smeared as a "bigot," "a hater" and "homophobe" by the ever-"intolerant left", for the 'question' of gender in society is an affront to Holy Scripture, beginning in the garden. Note Genesis 3":

> *When the woman saw that the fruit of the tree was good for food and pleasing to the eye, and also desirable for gaining wisdom, she took some and ate it. She also gave some to her husband, who was with her, and he ate it. Then their eyes were opened, and they realized they were naked. Genesis 3:6-7*

Dr. King smiled as he continued: While still fighting the battle I noted as I examined the Scriptures, that I learned that the discovery of human nakedness, second to Calvary's Cross, is the Creator's greatest gift to humanity. It is through this modesty that a protected family life evolved. It is painfully obvious that our society in general has placed its 'stamp of approval' upon this grievous practice. Homosexual relationships demonstrate sin against God. Crimes against personality, and offences against humanity.

I Love You Lord – Ron

Reaching My Endurance

As I walked along Glory's streets my thoughts recalled an earlier time. A day when it was surmised that I was at Heaven's Door.

Dear Jesus

Just before lunch I reached my endurance. With some difficulty, and with Elaine's assistance, I made it to the car, expecting to get some meds from our family doctor. Arriving at the doctor's office, the nurse motioned for me to bypass the filled waiting room and led me into the examining room. The doctor took one look at me, after checking my vitals, instructed; "I want you to go to the emergency immediately". By the reception I received upon arriving at the hospital, I assumed that my doctor had called ahead as I was approached by an attendant with a wheelchair and taken directly to Intensive Care.

When my heartbeat dropped into the high twenties, it was determined that a pace-maker was in order and, an ambulance took me to an Edmonton hospital where an intensive care nurse never left my side. Through the night, my heart returned to normal. Thankyou Lord for your answer to those many prayers. As the ambulance attendants were wheeling me out of the room for my transfer back to Lloydminster, an R.N. stopped them and asked; "You've been such a great patient, can I give you a hug?" Thank You Jesus. I Love You Lord – Ron

God is NOT My Co-Pilot

Dear Jesus, this morning as usual, I asked that you guide me through the day. The day was unfolding as usual, I drove the fifty kilometres to visit my mother in Hospital – After my visit "I started home. Suddenly I felt a strong urge to "TAKE THE OTHER ROAD" Ignoring the "urge" I turned onto highway 14. Then within a few minutes, THAT URGE became stronger. There was just "something about it" Turning in a laneway, I headed back into town and took the old gravel road home. What happened? A major accident on the highway? – actually, NOTHING, nothing at all. But as I began my day asking for Your guidance, only You knew what might have happened. I really feel it was Your leading that caused me to alter my path today. Did You save me from something? Did You Lord? – perhaps this side of Glory I may never know.

Lord, this morning I recalled a car bumper "God Is My Co-Pilot"; causing a stirring in my soul. Lord You are not Co- anything with me! You are in control. I asked You to guide me through the day. I will trust You wherever You take me. When I was touched by a compulsion to take the different road, even though it didn't make sense to me. You being my pilot for today and always, it's incumbent upon me to accept whatever path You choose for the day. Lord, help me to always be ready follow Your leading.

I love You Lord – Ron

Congregational Worship

Dear Jesus:

While it is apparent that all of Christendom subscribes to the Biblical teaching and emphasis of an incorporation of Biblical Holiness and Biblical Love. An 'investigative worshipper' will find that a leaning toward HOLY produces a liturgical stance while a leaning toward LOVE produces a greater charismatic stance. Of particular note is that multitudes find salvation and fullness of worship in every blending of Love/Holiness by the inspiration of the Holy Spirit.

My tracing of the 'culture' of the Anglican, Baptist, Free Methodist, Lutheran, Mennonite, Pentecostal, Presbyterian, Roman Catholic and United Church of Canada (in my opinion) supports my hypotheses concerning the ratio of love/holiness as established in formal worship, implanted within the church fathers and mothers the different structures of worship by the Holy Spirit. Church history is well documented that no combination is superior to the other. Thus for example, we are brought into the family of God via Pentecostalism, Free Methodism, Anglicism, Roman Catholicism or United Churchism etc etc.

Through much evaluation, I have reached a hypothesis that the ratio of Love/Holiness decides where a family finds a place of worship.

	Love	**Holy** (ness)
Anglican	40%	60%
Baptist	60%	40%
Free Methodist,	60%	40%
Lutheran CALK	38%	62%
Lutheran ELCIC	35%	65%
Lutheran Missouri	30%	70%
Mennonite	55%	45%
Pentecostal,	80%	20%
Presbyterian	45%	55%
Roman Catholic,	20%	80%
United Church,	65%	35%

As previously alluded; Church history is well documented that no one combination is superior to the other. Then too, the power of the Holy Spirit transcends human attempts to confine bonified worship into a cauldron of spirituality in accordance with one's personal desires.

Ron Hobden

Meeting of Satan's Demoniacs

As we admired our surroundings, passing by vast multitudes of saints, for all here in Glory are "saints", knowing all about the joys and anguished lives, but never the pain, each experienced prior to their arrival here in the 'promised land" I commented to brother Bob how in times past, Satan had called for the grand council of Hades to determine how they might bring spiritual ruination to the souls of mankind. It was at a meeting after much deliberation that Satan approved the release of his hordes to plant the 'seed' of "There's No Hurry" Into the hearts of mankind whenever one's thoughts considered turning their soul over to Jesus; that there was 'no hurry.' This concept was working well, persuading countless that while they needed a Saviour there was no need to make an immediate decision. Yet, even with the great success of this strategy, Satan's impatience was growing. A second council was convened.

It was determined that the "No Hurry" plan was serving well. As the meeting was to conclude, once again Hell's most evil angel, approached the Satanic throne. "And what would you have us do to further induce mankind to enter our eternal domain." The most evil angel responded. "My prince, our 'No Hurry' campaign is bearing much fruit, and we need to sustain it. However, I believe that we should add one extra tool to our war-chest." "And what do you have in mind? Satan inquired." To which the satanic replied. In addition to our No Hurry Campaign. I urge we consider Inter-Racial Hatred. In the name of Christianity, a universal blossoming of hatred between Jews and Gentiles could flourish. So it would be, that hatred could also form between Catholics and Protestants, eastern and western societies. Indeed, wherever we find an assembly of man to foster a hatred of their fellow man."

Again, Satan paused for a moment as he had done at the proposal of the No Hurry matter. Then with a broad smile he said; "I like it, but let's add the 'joy of same-sex relationships.' I place my legions to aide you. GO, GO"

Time passed, then Satan called again for his minions' presence. The very presence of the chief of demons quivered as he reported; "You have done your job. I can now predict that Kings could be vanquished; A president of a thousand lies could bring his country to collapse. Factions such as an American far-right, neo-fascist, organization, The Proud Boys that can promote and engage in political violence is even now hard at work for us we must prepare more space in the fires of hell to accommodate our ever growing numbers.

You're sowing of the seeds of racial hatred either directly or indirectly birthed this profound anti holiness upon the earth. Satan beamed as he reiterated; our interracial hate campaign has already spawned innumerable side issues.

To counter this war, the arch angel Gabriel, accompanied by vast multitudes of angels, had descended upon the earth to strengthen the hearts and minds of the committed and empower those on the brink, to a holy committal, to implant within the hearts and minds of the weak followers an offering of absolute assurance that they are never alone never without help. God's love for them is unfailing, it never stops, it is eternal. God's love is the very reason they are alive. The more they become rooted and grounded in God's love, the more they will become happy, fruitful and fulfilled.

Counselled by the Holy Spirit, to place the prayer from Ephesians in receptive hearts;

God's love is very personal toward them. It doesn't matter where they've been, it doesn't matter what they've done, it doesn't matter what they've experienced - God loves them. It doesn't matter what they thought about themselves or what other people may have said about them - God loves them. The are precious in their heavenly Father's eyes. Yet as a great prophet considered; *"The harvest is past, the summer has ended, and they remain unsaved."*

Jeremiah 8: 20

Crying Out in Distress

Dear Jesus

I voiced as I paused my thought. The doctor's office called this morning. Oh Lord, what new challenges are before me? I know that my future is in Your Hands, but Lord the words of from Psalm 107 shows my weakness. Lord as I consider the possibilities of my future, I too cry out to You in my distress.

'When O Lord will you still my storm to a whisper? When will You still the waves about me?" Then; from your Word, I recalled:

> *Listen! I have carried you since you were born; I have taken care of you from your birth. Even when you are old, I will be the same. Even when your hair has turned grey, I will take care of you. I made you and will take care of you. I will carry you and save you.* Isaiah 46:3-4

Ron Hobden

I do love You Lord. I believe, but Lord, help my unbelief. - During the next few hours my struggle continued, I recalled a writer's words.

> *"When the raging winds and tempest, And the noxious clouds of sin, Whirl around me like an army, And my faith is wearing thin, In a whispering distant thunder, Comes a voice like morning calm: "Fear not, I am with you ever, Till the world shall see its end"*

Richard W. Adams

Oh Jesus, I desperately need to feel your presence. I Love You Lord - Ron

The Cancer Clinic

Dear Jesus

With an afternoon's phone call, I was to learn I'd face a new challenge. The tests were in, The doctor's next words: I'd like to see you soonest, and have Elaine accompany you". "That really got my attention." Elaine took my hand and we knelt in prayer before our Lord.;

> *"Heavenly Father, we know that You are close to those who seek You. Give us a revelation of Your presence, please give us a special tangible sense that You are here. In the name of Jesus, strengthen Ron not to fear this illness, for the finished work of Christ is working in us. Your presence is heaven to us.*

As we entered the doctor's office, "Mr. Hobden, I'm sorry to have to tell you that it's a cancer. BUT, of all cancers; Follicular non-Hodgkin's Lymphoma is one of the tamest."

As you are at Stage 3, I recommend we follow the standard prescribed format. That will require you to attend the Cancer Clinic every month for the next year. Your cancer is not curable, but manageable. Most manage a normal lifestyle." I could see that Elaine wanted to ask the next obvious question but hesitated. "Dr. what about life expectancy?" "I can say with some certainty, it should have no bearing."

We love You Lord – Ron

Comfort in the Cancer Clinic

Dear Jesus:

Wednesday was my first visit to the Cancer centre. Lord, there were so many people waiting for their summons to treatment. We were all there for serious and life-threatening conditions. Yet there was calm in the room. I was surprised at what I saw. My surprise soon ended as I was summoned to a treatment chair. The kindness, the comfort, the understanding of the caring nurses seemed to be above and beyond the call of service. My apprehension gave way to assurance. Thank you, Lord, for directing me to this place of care. As I left the Cancer Centre, I recalled an interchange the day before with the doctor; "Mr. Hobden, I've noticed that you are upbeat most of the time." "Well". I commented, "Somewhere I learned that it takes less energy to smile than to frown." Nodding, he answered, "With that attitude, you're going to beat this thing." Lord, thank you, as this storm envelops me You remind me that most face the storms of life. I know that these storms include disappointment and illness, Yet, thank you that You are beginning to still my storm.

I Love You Lord – Ron

One Last Time

Dear Jesus:

Due to the onset of my cancer, this morning, I stood behind my pulpit for the last time. Should, in the future, I have the privilege of again preaching the Word, it will be at the invitation of a pastor to do so. Lord, over the sixty years of my ministry, You provided me with the honour of preaching Your Word in: Canada, the U.S. the U.K. and Japan, and even on a cruise ship midway between Vancouver and Hawaii. In churches with forty pews and others with thousands. I recalled the opportunity of teaching religious education, of opening your word at many dozens of funerals, numerous weddings, baptisms, confirmations. In seniors' residences, provincial jails, and, above all Lord, you have opened the way for me to lead so many to You for their personal salvation.

My cancer is uncurable, yet I should enjoy life for years. How many? A number I must leave in Your hands. But Lord, grant, I ask, that You will bless me with some form of ministry on into the future. As I paused my writing for a few moments, You reminded me of the Psalmist's words:

> *I will instruct you and teach you in the way you should go; I will counsel you with my loving eye on you.* Psalm 32:8 NIV

I Love You Lord – Ron

HE Repaired Our Car

Dear Jesus:

For our 61st wedding anniversary. The family presented us with a gift of cash and a suggestion that we would enjoy a couple of days at a hot spring. At the end of our time at the resort, I backed into a low post. There was a large depression in our right rear bumper. The cost of repair would certainly strain our savings. We asked, our Lord for guidance. Just what should we do? Uncharacteristically I put off heading over to a body-shop. Days then weeks passed. I just didn't feel as though I should have the damage repaired. I must admit Lord, that 'putting things off', just wasn't my norm.

One afternoon as we were walking past the car I stopped. At that moment, words would not come. All signs of damage were gone. The thousand dollar "bump" was 'repaired'! Later, I discovered that hot rays from the sun MAY have caused the plastic to expand, returning the bumper to its former shape.

O Lord, how often over the years have I stood behind Your pulpit and preached from Matthew 19; for people in desperate situations; crippling illness, loss of loved ones, financial ruin, churches facing closure, "With God all things are possible." But Lord, I never imagined that Your 'care' included repairing a fender on my car. I do believe, but Lord, help my unbelief.

I love You Lord – Ron

A Place to Worship

Dear Jesus

Having moved to Saskatoon it was priority that we settle in a new church home as quickly as possible. That should have been an easy transition as the denomination that ordained us and for whom we served as pastors for many years had two congregations in the city. As our understanding of holy writ invoked a low tolerance toward certain sexual issues and having heard unsubstantiated rumours about the larger of the two churches, I decided to put the question to the pastor. The call went something like this;" Hi pastor, my wife and I have just moved into the city and are looking for a place to worship, could you advise about your church's views on same-sex marriages?" "Well, Ron if you go onto Google and bring up this past week's sermon focusing on the 'joys of same sex unions" it should fill you in."

Now Lord, as the denomination, had a second church in the city and our information concerning it seemed more promising, we decided that we'd just attend for Sunday worship.

Ron Hobden

As the Sunday "program" proceeded it appeared to us that there was a significant lack of preparation. At the end of this 'event' as we drove away, I asked Elaine' Did you hear of even one verse of scripture read or quoted? My wife confirmed that it wasn't due to the setting of my hearing aids that I missed any reference to God's Holy Word as not even a single verse was read or even quoted. Even the benediction was 'unique", "You can go home now, we have a meeting." Over coffee, I asked a daughter, a former pastor, if she had suggestions. She replied that her family was attending a church nearby that really didn't meet their expectations of worship and they were searching for a new church home but they would continue to support and attend until their search was successful. Knowing that we felt a need of corporate Sunday worship, she suggested we could visit the coming Sunday. Arriving at the church, we were warmly welcomed. While I found it necessary to turn both hearing aids off, finding the music while repetitious, was to me bearable. Then by actual count 'Amen' was repeated 17 times. Then after an excellent message, it was time for Children's Moments. The children and a couple of adults joined the two leaders on stage in the hopping around, waving arms, being altogether at times ultra charismatic. Later in the weeks that followed the question was often raised; "Any idea what the target age was for kiddies' moments?" "Well last Sunday we thought teens, today possibly Bible Teachers." The pastor's message offered for a blessing throughout the week. Although I did feel that the band was lacking bag pipes and taped claps of thunder.

One afternoon, I received a call from a pastor I had supervised during his study toward ordination. Suggesting that we contact a Pastor Scott; a pastor perhaps sharing more to our concept of "worship". A welcome was extended to us with an invitation to their service at Reflection Ministries where we found a warm, caring and serving congregation.

Months have now passed. An incident arose last Sunday portraying the pastor's sharing the caring love of his Saviour. Assisting in the serving of holy communion, I made my way to the front. Trailing behind me a noisy trio of young children. Pastor Scott took in the situation. Without curt instructions for the kiddies interrupting the service. Instead with a smile welcomed them and said, come let's have a prayer before you return to your seats. The pastor and I reached out to the children's outstretched hands as the pastor offered a prayer of thanksgiving for the children. Then at his suggestion, they returned to their seats. Nods and smiles of appreciation radiated from a congregation who thanked their Lord for the pastor's ability to share the Saviour's love with the children while maintaining a sense or worship within the sanctuary. Lord, your words from Matthew 19 "Let the little children come to me, and do not hinder them, for the kingdom of heaven belongs to such as these." flowed well into my heart.

I Love You Lord – Ron

God is HOLY -
God is LOVE

Sometimes here in Glory I attempt to explain the wonders of my Heavenly mansion in what might be earthly terms, Yet there are simply no words of human comprehension that could manage the task. As I considered another question of human/Christian reality. 'Why did the apostle Paul's ministry evolve into the dozen or so leading denominations and their numerous 'offshoots'?

One of the early church's saintly leaders appeared at my side. Although we had never been introduced, and were born thousands of years apart, I knew everything relevant to his dedication for his Lord. I gave a welcome smile to Barnabas.

Barnabas a Levite from Cyprus one of the church greats who led not only Jews but many Gentiles to the Christian faith. identified in Acts 11:24 as "a good man, full of the Holy Spirit and faith" who brought "a great number of people ...to the Lord. As I knew Barnabas' life history and even his present thoughts, so he knew mine. He smiled then countered, I see you're back at the Holiness/Love conundrum again. Seems to me that you covered the topic pretty well. It's all in your diary. See now your research; You wrote:

Dear Jesus: I'm struggling with my latest research; "The emergence of Christianity." The Bible is clear —"God is HOLY, God is LOVE". And Lord as I understand You are Holy, meaning:

You are set apart from anything or anyone on this planet. And because You are holy You desired us to be holy too. "As it is written, *"You shall be holy, for I am holy.""* – 1 Peter 1:16 "And Lord You demonstrated Your own love for us in this: *While we were still sinners, You died for us.* Romans 5:8. As I consider those two statements - BOTH clearly developed in Holy Writ, I'm reaching what I consider an interesting hypothesis; While it is apparent that all of Christendom subscribes to the Biblical teaching and emphasis of an incorporation of Biblical Holiness and Biblical Love, it appears to me that the 'balance' of the two (holiness and love) defines where the church's denominationally, congregationally and individually stand in their approach to worship.

A heavier leaning toward HOLY produces a greater liturgical stance conversely, a heavier leaning toward LOVE produces an increased greater charismatic stance. My tracing of the "culture" of the Anglican, Baptist, Free Methodist, Lutheran, Lutheran CALK, Mennonite, Pentecostal Presbyterian Roman Catholic, United Church and others, appears to support my hypothesis concerning the ratio of love/holiness in the established forms of worship: In my personal opinion – without solid established and comprehensive study, for my personal evaluation, I unscientifically determined the following:

	Love	Holy
Anglican	35%	65%
Baptist	50%	50%
Free Methodist,	55%	45%
Lutheran CALK	40%	60%
Lutheran ELCIC	35%	65%
Lutheran Missouri Synoid	30%	70%
Mennonite	55%	45%
Pentecostal,	75%	25%
Presbyterian	45%	55%
Roman Catholic,	20%	80%
United Church of Canada,	60%	40%
Queen Elizabeth's Funeral	15%	85%

The relationship between love and holiness in the history of the church is checkered. It's tempting to characterize churches as veering into the ditch on one side of the road or the other. Either they have veered too far toward holiness and separation, thereby forsaking love, or they have veered too far toward love and assimilation, thereby forsaking holiness. Some churches have veered too far toward what *they think* is holiness, while other churches have veered too far toward what *they think* is love. If a church has abandoned holiness, it has abandoned love, and if it has abandoned love, it has abandoned holiness. Holiness and love are mutually implicated and work in concert, not in opposition. GOD'S HOLINESS IS HIS LOVE

My Dwelling

As my sister Fran and I were exploring the heavenly expanse of my dwelling, we were discussing a theologian's calculation that the Holy City would be the approximate size of the moon. Whereupon we calculated that from creation to this period of earthly time, there would have been one hundred billion souls on our earth but only twenty percent would have accepted the King's invitation of personal salvation. I recalled that while in my earthly body I often thought of the millions of souls that would standing before the Cross in judgement, hear the King's verdict, "Depart from me, I never knew you."

Joining us, grandpa Hobden spoke up; 'Ron, I recall a significant moment when King Jesus was indeed watching over you. Again, my diary opened:

Dear Jesus

Thank you for touching Ken's heart!

As I marvelled in wonder at the great street of the city under my feet, Ken appeared at my side. He was the man of God who opened the way for me as a young teenager.

Ken travelled from his farm to our community at his own expense, to introduce us to Jesus. I never recalled an offering collected or a request for assistance to support this ministry. We gazed in absolute rapture as we took in the wonder before us. Ken whispered; "This is described in the Book of Revelation's description 'as of pure gold like transparent glass', but as we look at this', he pointed to the path upon which we were walking, this is far beyond the ability of the human eye to comprehend." 'Ron', Ken, interrupted, "I recall the moment that you gave your heart to the Saviour. The joy I felt at that moment covered a hundred times the price of my travel. Weeks later you, let me read an entry from your diary. On this side of the gate I recall every word.

It was the early fall of 1954. You and your mother walked from your home on the farm to the school. As I recall there were about ten to fifteen folk from the surrounding farms that usually attended the meeting. The service progressed to the sermon. In those days we preachers spoke from the King James version, yet, the Lord had His hand upon you and as the words from Timothy were spoken you heard with clarity; Let no man despise thy youth;

Jesus was saying; "I know that you are young, that doesn't matter, I have a future for you. Now think like a man. Whenever anyone calls you a child, just remember you are MY child, if you allow me to accompany you, you will have experiences beyond your imagination." You sat through the message enthralled by God's words. As the service ended, you slipped out of the school and in the darkness, you found your Jesus and He touched your soul. As always, true to His word, King Jesus led you through years, decades, of wonder, beginning with your winning public speaking contests, then at the tender age of seventeen, a church with enough confidence in you, appointed you as supply to their seven-point summer charge.

Your service for the King would throughout the coming decades takes you to congregations throughout Canada, the United States, The U.K. and more than a decade of service in Japan where you would come to be enraptured with the faith of Luis Ibaraki, one of the twenty-six Nagasaki martyrs in 1597. He was the youngest, only 12 years old.

On his way to his crucifixion, he was told by a samurai to give up his belief in order to escape dying on the cross. Ibaraki responded to him, "It would be better if you also became a Christian and joined me on the way to heaven." Luis Ibaraki's life portrayed a 'no turning from service to King Jesus. Unknowingly I was adapting this philosophy. This became apparent one Sunday.

I opened my Bible to my sermon theme. Glenn now a progressive four-year-old, well acquainted with our code of conduct during worship, demanded a crayon from his older sister and at the moment Elaine was with me up front.

Julie shook her head in refusal at which Glenn began yelling; "I want" I paused in my reading and motioned to my son to be quiet. To no avail. Leaving the pulpit I picked the child up, placed him across my knee, then administered a firm swat on the seat of his pants. To the nods of approval, I returned to the pulpit.

I am convinced that it was through Elaine's and my approach to parenting, our eldest daughter Julie Ann, became a young people's leader, David and Brent administrators for the Salvation Army, Glen and wife Shirley became pastors,

Daughter Lara a pastor and Dennis a well-respected teacher in construction.

Lord, not one of our seven children nor their spouses have ever been before a court, required treatment for drugs or alcoholism. Yet there, before the cross stand countless souls waiting their turn. There they watch as every incident where they failed in their responsibility as parents to their children appears before them. Then they see "What could have been but was never to be, because of their parental neglect."

Dear Saviour, thus far, the Supreme Court of Canada has permitted spanking for certain ages of unruly children. However as one considers the near future, only You know the ramifications for parents tapping their unruly kiddies on their bottom.

Lacking Faith

Dear Jesus:

Two angels were discussing the lack of faith upon the earth. Seeing my interest, I was invited to join them. In the distance I could see disturbance outside the Gate. Are these all destined for the lower region?" I asked. "Only the Judge knows". YET, consider the clear unmistakable guideposts to eternal Life:

"Look there" an angel motioned. There a collection of men and women who were once pastors of the Word and Sacrament, over there, Sunday school teachers, there leaders in their congregations. Before us: the Elderly, teens, youngsters, all facing the reality of their past existence.

Looking upon their Saviour's face we see His smile and nods. Following their judgement, they shall be brought into the Kingdom. Then we see tears flowing down His face as it is revealed to others the consequences of how their neglect, their words, their actions their lack of love was responsible for denying those in their care the right to pass through the gate. There, politicians, who had abused the trust of their constituents using their office for illicit personal gain. Those who were compulsive liars, those who came to power by spreading false rumours against their political foes. Those charged with providing care for residents in personal care homes who betrayed their codes of conduct mistreating those under their care. There, countless individuals – too busy to accept Salvation.

THERE: children who had reached their level of discernment to know right from wrong yet, rebelled against home and parents.

THERE; a teen who had succumbed to a fatal disease. Months before during the threat of covid, she was required to wear a mask during school attendance. She chose a mask that was meaningful to her. One that expressed her faith.

You are aware of course that her mansion is but an instant from yours." Nodding, "I see her often."

Lydia's classmates seemed to have the same idea. Students wore masks displaying Black Lives Matter, and several other slogans. So, imagine Lydia's surprise when school officials forced her to remove her mask because it read; Jesus loves me, a statement unacceptable on school property. Here in Glory, we await the moment when those school officials stand awaiting their judgement. One can only anticipate that their judgement shall include the warning of Saint Matthew's words:

> *"If anyone causes one of these little ones—those who believe in me—to stumble, it would be better for them to have a large millstone hung around their neck and to be drowned in the depths of the sea.*

I Love You Lord – Ron

It All Began

Appearing before me, my mother reminded me of what became trivial when it really was, as my diary recorded; "My life history all hinged upon a grade ten assignment way back at least way back THEN, to 1956. Each student was to give a three minute speech. I was petrified." Then, as my diary concludes, I'm approached by an angel. He responds: "Praise be to our Lord of Lords and King of Kings. Some of those teen students you worked with during your stint with M.A.P.S. have accepted the Saviour. They are here with us, COME, rejoice in their presence.

For the next few hours earth time but – milli-seconds here in Glory, joined by my father I stood in wonderous joy before the throne marvelling at the angelical choir's hymn of praise. Upon the final 'amen', dad broke the silence; "Ron. While you didn't understand at the time, lessons learned during your childhood on the farm may have seemed harsh, however it was through many of those difficult times that our Lord permitted them for the spiritual and intellectual growth of the family. Lessons that would go toward the equipping you for your family and pastoral service."

We took in the wonders of this, our forever home with the King and the angelic host. As dad was about to respond to a call, he concluded this first of what would surely be a vast multitude of future 'togetherness' Ron, he put forward, "Let me suggest that your service to the King all began when as a fourteen year old teenager you won a grade ten speaking event.

A few weeks later the church young people met to organize Youth Service Sunday. Jina would sing a solo. Tom the announcements. Bill to read the scripture selections. Karla would serve as prayer leader. Then the sermon. Garnet piped up; what about Ronny? Having won the town public speaking event, you were the unanimous choice. The youth service was well received, with many compliments. Following service as Mr. Massie shook my hand, "Well done Mr. Hobden You should consider entering the ministry." That was really the first time anyone referred to me as Mr. Hobden and most definitely my first call to ministry. About a month later Mr. Massie approached me on the street. With extended hand; "Mr. Hobden, your part in the youth service, again, well done. As you probably know we are searching for a minister. Rev Franks is retiring the end of the month. We do have a student arriving in a couple of weeks, but our seven point charge is just too much for a seminary student to manage. Our committee feels that if we could split the work in two it would be manageable. Our student has agreed to our plan. One Sunday he would conduct services in four churches, the next Sunday the other three.

Now, we were wondering. Would you be interested in taking on the other half of the services for three months? If you might be willing to accept this challenge our committee will first meet with your parents so that everything will be above board." As I was about to say "No thankyou", A thought came to mind, "If I say no, what will Aunt Sara say"? This strange request was granted by my parents. Thus, I began a seven week stint as 'pastor' for the parish. So it was that Kenneth and I divided the seven point charge consisting of: Nairn, Massey, Walford, Spanish, Webwood, High Falls and Lee Valley.

One Sunday Kenneth would preach at four of the churches and I the other three. The following Sunday I took on the four and Kenneth the three. Not an easy challenge for a seminary student and almost beyond belief for a seventeen-year-old kid, but the Lord was with both of us. I prepared for each Sunday before the days of computers, long before printers, reference books were few and far between. Dear Lord, there wasn't even a library on our pastoral charge. Somehow through it all Kenneth survived the summer, returned to seminary, in time graduated and went on to take on the coveted title of Reverend. It was only by the guidance of The Holy Spirit that I so enjoyed that summer. Then ten years later I was to return to a pastorate. The words of William Cowper's hymn seems to sum up it all:

> *God moves in a mysterious way, His wonders*
> *to perform; He plants his footsteps in the sea,*
> *And rides upon the storm.*

I Love You Lord – Ron

Dr. Elaine Hobden   Dr. Ronald Hobden

Printed in the United States
by Baker & Taylor Publisher Services